Praise for *Rest, Girl*

Many of us are bad at resting, and I am the chief of sinners. This is why I'm thankful for Jami Amerine's reminder that God invites us to a life of rest. This book is not an invitation to take a momentary breather; it's a clarion call to change the posture of your life from one of worry to rest. As always, Jami Amerine's writing is full of honesty and humor. She has experienced her fair share of storms, which makes her the perfect person to write about the One who slept through storms and empowers us to do the same. Why be ruled by worry when you can rule from rest?

-Paul Ellis, Author of *The Silent Queen: Why the Church Needs Women to Find their Voice and Stuff Jesus Never Said*

Rest, Girl is a must read! Jami Amerine knows firsthand what it feels like to crawl through each day, exhausted and weary. And yet, through life experience, the study of scripture, and a deep affection for Jesus, she has learned a better way. A way that leaves her energized, filled with hope, and eager to share what she has found with others—the way to true rest. Filled with hilarious anecdotes and heart-stirring truth, *Rest, Girl* offers laughter and hope to your weary soul, and a promise that a life of rest and joy is truly possible.

-Jennifer Bleakley, author of *Joey: How a Blind Rescue Horse Helped Others Learn to See and Pawverbs: 100 Inspirations to Delight an Animal Lovers Heart*

I value friends who speak hard truths *into* me while praying peace and blessing over me. Jami Amerine is one such friend to me! As you read the following pages filled with what her own heartache, faith journey, and research has taught her, I imagine Jami will become a truth-speaking, peace-praying friend of yours too! In *Rest, Girl*, Jami helps weary women like us to finally understand why we have never truly been at rest, even though we love God and trust His promises. Via her trademark mix of wit and humor, you'll come to see that chronic unrest happens whenever our words and thinking do not line up. Allow Jami to show you how true rest can be your reality going forward whenever you take God at His Word; receiving His love over the fears and lies that have kept your mouth and mind wound up and misaligned for years.

-Tracy Steel, mentor, speaker, and author of
A Redesigned Life: Uncovering God's Purpose When Life Doesn't Go As Planned

Like Jami, I have struggled with a "What If Ugh" mindset, assuming the worst and rehearsing hurts, which has resulted in unrest. After reading *Rest, Girl* I am consciously choosing to adopt a "What If Wow" mindset, asking myself, "What if this goes well? What if there is no longer a disconnect between what I profess and how I live? What if it is possible to daily embrace the Good News of the Gospel and walk in the freedom and peace Jesus died to give us?" *Rest, Girl* will make you think and it will stretch you, while simultaneously inviting you to rest in the goodness of God. . .not buts.

-Katie M. Reid, author of *Made Like Martha* and
A Very Bavarian Christmas, and co-founder of
ChangeYourMindChangeEverything.org

What would it feel like if the rumbling in your heart stilled like the storm Jesus spoke to? What if your shoulders lowered out of your ears? What if your mind stopped racing? You would feel the rest Jesus promised. Jami repeatedly points us back to Christ as we wrestle with what leaves us exhausted and stressed. It's time rest in the blessing. Read on, dear one!

-Jill E. McCormick, co-author of *Sister, Walk in Truth*
and host of the *Grace In Real Life* podcast

FOREWORD BY
SUSANNAH B. LEWIS

Rest, Girl

A JOURNEY
FROM EXHAUSTED AND STRESSED
TO ENTIRELY BLESSED

Jami Amerine

Print ISBN 978-1-63609-066-5

eBook Editions:
Adobe Digital Edition (.epub) 978-1-63609-233-1

Published by Barbour Publishing, Inc., 1810 Barbour Drive, Uhrichsville, Ohio 44683, www.barbourbooks.com

Our mission is to inspire the world with the life-changing message of the Bible.

Printed in the United States of America.

For you, dear sister
in Christ. . .I love you.
You are seen and known.
Welcome to rest.

Contents

Foreword

Jami Amerine is my friend, so when she asked me to write the foreword for *Rest, Girl*, I agreed without hesitation. I'll be honest though; I thought of it as an assignment. It was merely an assignment with a deadline that I penciled on my calendar just like dozens of other writing assignments I've had in my career.

I planned to get through a few chapters over morning coffee and pen some nice words for her readers. My duty was to get people jazzed over the book. That was it. That was the task at hand.

But, before my first cup of coffee was gone, reading Jami's words no longer became a task. Reading this book wasn't merely preparation for writing the foreword. Her words spoke to me. They spoke life into me. They spoke rest, relief. The new task at hand wasn't to come up with a couple of paragraphs for you. It was to grow, to understand, to seek this Jesus Jami so lovingly speaks of.

As a child, I thought of Jesus as a greater being who lived somewhere in the clouds above the water tower in my small, southern town. Jesus and His Father both looked down on me—and I mean that in more ways than one. They looked down on me—the despicable, chubby bully who stole grapes from Kroger—the way a stern, disappointed teacher looks down on a student sitting at a desk with a cheat sheet.

Jesus looked down on me when I used bad words and lied to keep myself out of trouble. God looked down on me when I was a drunken teenager puking Boone's Farm in a cotton field. Father and Son were just waiting to throw a bolt of lightning my way.

But finally, I understood grace the way Jami describes it in her book. I understood that Jesus was holding on to me when I wasn't holding on to Him. Jesus really loved me—the flawed, disgusting, sinful me. This didn't excuse my sin, but it simplified it. It meant I didn't have to be bound to it. It meant I was worthy of forgiveness. It meant every drop of blood Jesus shed on the cross made me righteous.

I've known Jesus' beautiful, unchanging grace and mercy for a long time, but it still escapes me. When I've mucked up (again), I confuse conviction and condemnation. I'm overtaken by fear and worry. I get so distracted by all the negative voices coming at me that I forget the voice of Truth.

Before I sat down with coffee to read a couple chapters of *Rest, Girl*, I was struggling with some things—guilt and an elaborate plan B in case Jesus didn't come through.

But Jami did a beautiful (and often humorous) job of reminding me who Jesus really is and the attainable rest we can find through Him and Him alone.

Writing this foreword wasn't merely an assignment

after all. It was a blessing. Jami's book served as a powerful reminder of who Jesus really is, despite who I am or who I believe Him to be.

I know it will bless you too.

Susannah B. Lewis

Introduction

Sunday, 2:30 a.m.

I woke with a thought. . .

So, I googled the phrase "*Even if He doesn't.*"

I knew it was scripture, and I was right. It's from Daniel 3:18.

King Nebuchadnezzar demanded that everyone worship an idol or be thrown into a fiery furnace— three Hebrews refused. They claimed that God would save them, and even if He didn't. . .they would still believe.

And certainly, it is valid. Scripture always is. But I didn't know why it woke me from a dead sleep.

And then I thought, "Oh, it's a warning that He will not answer. . ."

But no.

That wasn't it.

It was doubt.

The habitual practice of unbelief and just cause to continue saying "I believe He will" and simultaneously doubting that He will. The faithless execution of worst-case scenarios and plan Bs if He doesn't come through, and I still must figure a way out of the predicament I'm in.

This is the uphill climb of limited faith, mindless worry, and want. And the exhausting battle of trying to understand Him and failing. Oh, me of little faith.

And still, I'd say I loved Him.

And still, I would announce His goodness.

But that's a practice in my faithfulness, not His. I will not deny Him.

What if instead of doubt, strife, and barely getting by until the next Sunday service, every day was laced with anticipation—*He does save, He did, He will, I trust?*

What if the mustard seed-size faith (Matthew 17:20) was the minimum standard, but I expected more of Him and trusted less in what I see and know?

What if "Help my unbelief!" was simply a breath on occasion instead of an endless, exhausting battle cry that defined this walk?

What if belief was so deeply steeped within me, water-walking, fire-dancing, and mountain-moving were common, and weariness, lack, and desperation were questionable? Even confusing?

What if the Sunday service to increase and encourage wasn't needed, and instead every sermon or lecture was testimony to the miraculous here and now? What if instead we only came to rest in worship not because He didn't or won't, but because He did and will?

What if instead of waiting up all night for Him to answer, we believed as if we already received?

What then would Sunday look like? How good would Monday be?

What if every day embodied the beautiful feelings of Sunday worship and wise company? That warm, life-giving emotion of God is everyone and everything?

What if I welcomed every day like Sunday?

Welcome, Tuesday.

How can this day be better?

How can tomorrow be the same excellent tribute in song and collection as Sunday?

If I needn't make excuses or try to make Him fit within the confines of what I can touch, feel, and see. . .

What if fishing for men wasn't about testifying to how greatly I "*kind of believe*" and how sometimes He shows up, but became a resounding gong of praise because. . .

He did. . .

He can. . .

He will. . .

He is. . .

I wonder, *what if*. . .

"Love turns work into rest."
TERESA OF ÁVILA

Part One

TOSSIN' AND TURNIN'

Chapter One

EXHAUSTED GIRL

"Come to me, all you who are weary and burdened, and I will give you rest."
MATTHEW 11:28

The store clerk ran screaming, "Stop! Shoplifter! Shoplifter!"

I stopped, hoping to lend assistance, although I don't know what kind. My eyes darted about the parking lot in search of a thief. A huge man, decked out in cowboy garb, grabbed my arm. Shocked and in utter disbelief, I winced as the dime-store, wannabe cattleman tightened his grip on my upper arm, nearly lifting me off my feet.

He was enormous, at least six foot five. His belly bulged over a hideous, dictionary-sized belt buckle I am certain he did not earn in a rodeo. The sun reflected off the gaudy keeper of his pants, blinding me. In dazed confusion, I pushed back at the wall of a man and yelped, "Take your hands off me!"

He spat stale tobacco chaw and barked, "You're going back inside to pay for that apple juice, missy!"

It took me entirely too long to recognize *I was the shoplifter.*

As the brute dragged me across the parking lot, the rail-thin, pimple-faced clerk in a polyester smock dialed his phone. "I gotta call in to the *poe-leese*, hold her! I gotta call the owner!"

Through tear-filled eyes, I read the branding on the clerk's smock: *Skinny's*.

Drenched in humiliation, I would now have to explain to the police and my husband's wealthy uncle, the owner of all the Skinny's convenience stores in the great state of Texas, I wasn't really shoplifting. I was just exhausted.

With three little ones at home impatiently waiting for apple juice and nausea chasing me from my latest surprise pregnancy, I had neither slept nor kept any food down in a month of Sundays. I should also note, all my pregnancies were a surprise. I am still surprised. I have a master's degree in human development, but Catholicism somehow trumped my comprehension of where babies come from. The only time I have not been surprised by the inception of motherhood was when we adopted our two youngest sons.

That I saw coming.

And while I hate to divulge too much and make my original batch of children question their arrival on the planet, I never got pregnant on purpose. The first time was a shock. The second time I believed I had a parasite from a recent trip to Venezuela. In all fairness, I was kind of right. Not that John is a parasite. But pregnancy does lend itself to the symbiotic life cycle. The third time I rationalized early menopause at the ripe old age of twenty-seven. And the fourth time I just sat on the floor and wept as my husband, Justin, stood over me waving a calendar and yelling, "There are no hearts! *NO HEARTS!*"

The hearts would have been indicative of conceptual possibilities on a "rhythm method" birth-control calendar we'd been encouraged to use in lieu of other forms of birth control not approved by the Catholic church. I would also like to add the rhythm method is still a form of controlling birth.

Unless you are the Amerines.

With calendar recording, or not recording; my teaching job at the university; a kindergartener; a hearing-disabled three-year-old; a disgruntled, non-sleeping two-year-old; and a side hustle managing my husband's and my house-building business, paying for apple juice seemed to have slipped my mind.

Things that did not slip my mind were the heavy burden of "have-tos." Those I had memorized. I knew I would now have to go to confession and explain my apple juice heist. Granted, I didn't really shoplift apple juice. But at that point in my life, every mistake, malady, or misfortune fell under the law of how badly I stank at the Christian walk.

Furthermore, I was drenched in the belief that God was trying to teach me something. And my lanta, He seemed like a mean and nasty teacher. As I drove home from Skinny's with paid-for apple juice in the seat next to me, I sobbed and begged the ruthless God of my head, a ruthless beast born of my beliefs, for mercy. That was immediately followed by the rote, out-loud formation of prayer-like words that chastised my existence.

"I should be more aware. I am such a ditz! I know I'm just awful! There are so many suffering humans. People that really must steal apple juice! I am ungrateful. I am disgusting. I am fat, lazy, and a horrible housekeeper. I know you are embarrassed by me. I don't know how I will ever pull it together! Also, I read the first three chapters of *Harry Potter*, which I know is the work of the devil."

It's not really, but I was young and religiously bound by fabricated works and unattainable standards.

I hiccup-sobbed my orthodox finale: "I am so sorry. Please, *please*. . .don't punish me. Amen." Then I performed the sign of the cross over myself seven times just to be safe.

Back at the ranch—literally, we lived on a ranch—I found a disheveled, exasperated Justin lying on the floor with too many children climbing on him, begging for apple juice. I slammed about the kitchen, still blubbering, and filled three sippy cups with once-stolen juice. Justin pried humans off himself, passed out the nectar, and then sheepishly inquired, "Rough trip?"

I filled clever, spill-proof snack cups with loopy cereal or fish-shaped snack crackers, I don't remember which. As I desperately tried to attach the tops to the snack cups, I flung snot and tears. I barely explained what had happened. Halfway through, out of sheer defeatist hunger, I popped three crackers in my mouth.

Five minutes later, I left Justin's consolation to throw up again.

Like sands through the hourglass, so were the days of my life.

A life that, many days, I wish I could do over. In my late forties, I'd like to think that I might have kicked the vigilante who nabbed me in the parking lot in the knee or otherwise. Then, to make my writing a bit more fragrant, perhaps I would have embraced the ensuing police chase. Like something out of *The Dukes of Hazzard*, I can see myself blazing over medians and whipping around other minivans in a reckless blaze of criminal apple juice acquisition and rebellious derision for the law.

Ah yes, the law.

Here is where I do not break the law as it is written, but instead I do not break the law for the Christ of my head is now the Jesus of my heart. It would be many years before I truly broke free. And while I sound tougher than I really am, my escape was more a gift than a tactical fugitive getaway.

I am not that precocious.

What I am is a people pleaser. I am a non-shoplifting, easily persuaded (hence the rhythm method debacles of 1995–2002), rule-following, list-making, grammar-checking, step-counting, reformed extrovert with obsessive tendencies for writing prose and painting daisies. I love my failed attempts at birth control. I adore the humans in my life. My husband is my best friend. My daddy is my biggest fan, and I am his. My kitchen talents are unmeasured, a pinch here and a dash there. I live 342 miles away from the ranch where I raised my four now semi-grown babies and a few thousand tears away from where I launched them into college, marriage, the Marines, and a Buddhist ashram (we can discuss that later).

But I am a million miles from who I was on the day I did not steal apple juice. I have loved well and lost better. I have chased and groveled. I have praised and complained. I have been transformed into a published author and professional artist. I've met with failure, rejection, success, betrayal, companionship, mercy, madness, and confusion. I am not the best sleeper, but I could win an Olympic medal for napping. Elvis would be proud.

Amid that lunacy, I met with Grace—the entire truth of who Jesus is and why He died. I remember everything about the day the scales fell from my eyes. I remember the phone call to my author friend, Katie M. Reid. I was standing in my bathroom looking out over 640 acres of rugged West Texas terrain. I stammered and struggled with the words, knowing, "She will think I'm crazy." Which I think she did and might still, but on that hot summer afternoon, as I stared out through lace panels and swollen eyes, I realized I could finally see.

I did not think it could get any better than learning about the freedom of Grace. Jesus' blood was the sacrifice that set us free. It was the perfect offering; it has no match. Exhaustion in our walk with the God who died is the systematic demolition of our righteousness through the belief that He must be paid back. It is the misguided and erroneous belief that we can earn the favor of our Father in heaven through good behavior. But more detrimental to all that we are in Him is the belief that we might lose Him for any reason, be it shoplifting or not.

If I'm honest, this is harder to write than I had expected, but so far removed from the prison cell of my old beliefs, it is almost impossible to recount what it felt like to read my Bible through cage bars. Every line dictated my wickedness. Each passage I read with the hope I would finally "get it." And every conversation, sermon, homily, class, seminar, and study was a desperate attempt to achieve that which I did not understand or grasp what I had already received.

To say I was tired, well, that would be a restrained characterization.

Are you bone tired? Does your mind feel foggy and your soul fatigued? I get it.

But might I suggest that more than restless nights and busy schedules, the source of exhaustion has more to do with our deep-seated beliefs and our mindset based on those well-intended beliefs?

And fear.

Fear is the ultimate thief of real rest.

I can say when I spy the law-bound, the spent, bone-weary believers, I recognize them quickly. So when they show their hand, by criticism of my work or a desperate plea for me to show them to the door, I'm racked with compassion. There is a part of me that wants to cry, "*It is right in front of us! Right here!*" But I also know I had the same information, and the world busied me, ironically with the same words that would eventually set me free.

And so, like them, I trudged in circles in my cell, too tired to try and too afraid not to.

Can you identify? Are you on the other side with me? Or have you sauntered up to the escape hatch but worried you might drown?

Truly, it doesn't matter which you said yes to. It has been five years since I encountered true Grace, but the ride only got wilder and simultaneously much more like a delightful nap in a hammock on a tropical beach.

Even after meeting with the Real Jesus, as documented in my first book, *Stolen Jesus*—I guess I kind of shoplifted Him. . .or more like brought Him into my home where He belonged—and falling headlong into His arms and freedom, I heard the words "There's more."

At first I thought, "Yep! I knew it. That had to have been too good to be true!" But no, there was more freedom.

More rest.

More to taste and see.

More tenderness, mercy, and guidance.

More abundance, peace, and joy.

More everything.

Perhaps after I wrote my third book, *Well, Girl*, I thought, "Well, I guess I get it now?" Laughable, that the depths of this God might be wholly uncovered in two hundred-ish pages or even in a lifetime, for that matter. No, this love is fantastic. Every day it is something bigger, bolder, grander! And yes, I know I sound like a criminally insane apple juice thief, but it is true.

I can't let you out of the cell, but I can tell you what I have experienced and help you pursue your escape.

Once you step out from behind the bars, we will rejoice, and, dear one, you will rest.

I also realize you might wonder, "What is more free than free?"

Well, girl: Wait until you hear this. . .

REST, GIRL REFLECTION

Trying hard or hardest to gain the love of God is like draining the ocean with a sieve. It is useless work; it will wear you out, and the effort cannot overcome the power of the waves.

DREAM JOURNALING

What would it look and feel like to understand the power of God's love? What "things" (worries, lies, etc.) have you believed? What is on your heavy list of "have-tos"?

Chapter Two

JUST BARELY

He replied, "Because you have so little faith. Truly I tell you, if you have faith as small as a mustard seed, you can say to this mountain, 'Move from here to there,' and it will move. Nothing will be impossible for you."
MATTHEW 17:20

Confusion and nonsense are the norms around the Amerine house. Sam, our second-youngest son, whom we adopted at nine days old, was born to parents of "Hispanic" descent. I use quotation marks because I don't understand the lumping of cultures. According to the Census Bureau, you need only call yourself "Hispanic" if you want to.[1] Sam's parents were not from Spain, Argentina, or Cuba. They were migrant workers from Mexico, which in my mind means that Sam is Mexican and should be proud to say so. Just as I would

1 Mark Hugo, Jens Manuel Krogstad, and Jeffrey S. Passel, "Who Is Hispanic," Pew Research Center, September 15, 2020, https://www.pewresearch.org/fact-tank/2020/09/15/who-is-hispanic/

never accept Scott-Irish-ic as a resolution to my heritage. I am always Scottish. Even on Saint Patrick's Day, when everyone declares themselves Irish, I am still Scottish. I take some pride in that heritage; it means something to me.

Despite the fact that we have always told Sam he is Mexican, not long ago at dinner he announced that he suspected he loved rice so much because he is Chinese. We all looked at him with collected confusion, and I said, "You are not Chinese, son. You are Mexican American." To which he replied, "I thought I was Chinese?" "No," I said.

And he questioned, "Hmmm, I wonder why I like rice so much then?"

Perhaps Sam loves rice because rice is just good stuff. It's an excellent vessel for butter, gravy, and soy sauce. But again, this is common practice confusion at our house. Further adding to the madness, our older children talk to each other in Australian accents. They are all quite good at it; however, I am ready for that trend to do a walkabout.

Charlie, the youngest of our six children, is an absolute riot. He sounds like he smokes a pack of cigarettes a day. That paired with his elaborate vocabulary makes him even funnier. I suppose his advanced lexicon was formulated from being raised around much older children in the home of a wordsmith. He says things like "Yes, yes, I quickly recognized that situation as suspicious." He also, for reasons we do not understand, says common British phrases such as "I need to go outside to play, *straight away*." He refers to his stuffed animals as "stuffies," and on occasion, he's been known to call me "Mum." Most recently he started saying, "Only just barely!"

"Mummy! I only just barely ate some of Sam's candy!"

Prior to his adoption into our family, Charlie was our first foster placement. I have known and loved him since he was three months old. He has never been across the pond, and we do not have cable. I don't know where the Brit in him bubbles up. It makes no sense. But much doesn't make sense in my life.

In one of the more confusing conversations with my children to date, Charlie had something black all over his nose. I mentioned it to him as he ran past me in the kitchen, "Charlie, you have something on your nose."

He quickly argued, "No, I don't!"

Ahhh, motherhood, it is indeed the opposite of rest. "Yes, you do, son," I explained. "I am looking at you. There is something black on your nose."

"What is it?" he asked.

I looked closer and said, "I think the stamp on your hand from the toy store rubbed off on your nose."

"What?" he again argued.

So, I expanded: "Your hand stamp rubbed off on your nose."

And Charlie, exasperated, said, *"I didn't do a handstand! I don't know how!"*

Fair and confusing enough.

Maybe it is the melting pot of nationalities, ages, lack of listening, and weirdness, but the festive blend of foreign slang, Aussie twang, and mistaken nationality for the love of rice left me thinking about the misunderstood word and the lost true identity of Christ.

How is it when we come to hear and know of this Jesus and the freedom of our salvation, we only just begin to delve into the exhaustive work of paying back the cross? Can you relate? Have you worked tirelessly to earn His love? Do you know what a huge feat it is? From volunteering to "perfect" motherhood, so many of us have beaten ourselves into the belief that every little thing we do counts for us or against us. Truly, the most perplexing tales in my journey to freedom and rest were the ones I imposed upon myself. Much like Sam, who somehow came to believe that he was Chinese, I left my baptismal bath, ignoring the promise and what I had been told, and went to work on being better. . . straight away.

And yes, I knew scripture. I understood the English translation, although not so much the King James Version. That is a bit more than my dyslexic brain can decode. But I won a prize from the Sunday school treasure box on more than one occasion for my mastery of scripture memorization.

You too?

Yes, it is a common practice among the "good ones." Know Thy Word. But what about the Word leaves us browbeaten and dead-dog tired, searching for more of Him and questioning the truth of who He is?

Honestly, I believe much of it has to do with how we read our Bibles. Starting from the beginning and working our way back only makes sense. That is how one reads a book. But what I have come to know is that the first half was to explain why we needed Jesus.

Jesus' life until His death was the explanation of why He would die.

Grace was best revealed to me when I understood, in nearly every case when Jesus was speaking, that He was speaking to the Law-bound Jewish community. And while He was a master wordsmith and parable sharer, He spoke to them about what was to come and how lost they would be should they stay behind. My people, the Scottish or Gentile community (yes, that was a joke, please tell me you knew that was a joke), were not even invited to Jewish law. The Jewish law was for the Jews. So, say you attend a Baptist church and they believe that dancing is wrong or a sin. You then move to attend a Disciples of Christ church, where dancing is permitted. Should you still abide by the Baptist church's law?

And while some have tried Jewish law or customs to experience what Jesus experienced, those acts should never be considered avenues to our salvation.

You don't have to observe the Passover to feast on the goodness of the Lamb; but if you want to observe it to experience what it was like, that's up to you. However, those rituals are no longer *required* nor do they tell us the finished story of the Lamb of God. They may point to our need for Him, but He is all we need—readily available to us without the need for us to eat of the bitter herbs of slavery any longer. He has come, and through His drinking of the cup of God's wrath for our sin, through His bitter death on the cross, we can be free indeed—resting from the toil of bondage and enjoying His company. Once and done, the blood worked. We are no longer bound to a performance-based salvation. Jesus was the answer to that problem. He didn't *just barely* save us. He saved us to the uttermost if we believe in Him (see Hebrews 7:25).

Hallelujah!

So, when today's believers read the Sermon on the Mount, in the first passages we hear the Good News. Everything we struggle with is blessed, intentionally cared for by the God who saves. Matthew 5:3–12 begins with the hope we now know because of Jesus. It reads:

> *"Blessed are the poor in spirit, for theirs is the kingdom of heaven.*
>
> *Blessed are those who mourn, for they will be comforted.*
>
> *Blessed are the meek, for they will inherit the earth.*
>
> *Blessed are those who hunger and thirst for righteousness, for they will be filled.*
>
> *Blessed are the merciful, for they will be shown mercy.*
>
> *Blessed are the pure in heart, for they will see God.*
>
> *Blessed are the peacemakers, for they will be called children of God.*
>
> *Blessed are those who are persecuted because of righteousness, for theirs is the kingdom of heaven.*
>
> *Blessed are you when people insult you, persecute you and falsely say all kinds of evil against you because of me. Rejoice and be glad, because great is your reward in heaven, for in the same way they persecuted the prophets who were before you."*

In verses 13 through 16 we learn about our vibrant faith. And then it gets confusing. Jesus speaks of the

Law and how it cannot be abolished. What I didn't understand then was that He was explaining that as long as you accepted the Law as your salvation, you had to abide by it perfectly. And after that, it gets ugly.

Matthew 5:21 on is scary—limbs cut off, eyes cut out, you can't even disagree with your sister or you face judgment! And this is where the words of Jesus confused me. The Sermon on the Mount, taught as if this were the standard, is impossible. I know now that was the point. The latter parts of this sermon are not referring to those who are believers in the resurrected Jesus. They are referring to those who were trying to be saved by the Law—through their works apart from Christ's finished work.[2] And if they were living under the Law? There are a few of us that should have already dug out an eye or cut off a limb—present company included.

From this place, I now see that Jesus was proclaiming how good it was to know and accept Him. But in the past, I had read the Bible through the shadowy vision of condemnation. And certainly, when Jesus is welcomed into our hearts, conviction will dictate that it is wrong to steal apple juice because it does not belong to us until we pay for it. Condemnation is an entirely different beast. And that beast will chase you in circles to make sure you are too tired to escape.

Furthermore, even after I stepped out of the prison cell of Law and into the banquet hall of Grace, I still was fatigued and confused as to why Jesus said some

---

2 Andrew Farley, "The Naked Gospel," video clip posted on Andrew Farley Ministries, accessed 03/03/2014, https://andrewfarley.org/audio_tag/sermon-on-the-mount/

of the things He said, and I did not experience them. If His yoke was easy, why was my back breaking from the load? I propose that it is more work from the dark side. And yes, that means I am saying that the world (enemy) uses the very Word of God against us. Very successfully, I might add.

And all the church ladies clutch their Bibles and gasp, "Oh my!"

Let me expound. I remember a church from my youth where the pastor shared a heated sermon about Matthew 4:21–44. Complete with a hanky, he wiped his brow and banged his fist on the pulpit. He raged on about our need to be perfect, and I remember thinking, "I better not ever mess up."

As members left the church, we stumbled out like zombies. We had been dealt with the heavy burden of the impossible, threats not meant for those in Christ. We were the walking dead. I watched out of the corner of my eye as the pastor was praised for his delivery of the much needed "truth."

Get it together or burn.

But more than just a creepy pastor or the cardinal sin of showing up to a potluck to eat and not bringing a tuna casserole to share, the enemy lurks not even in the shadows but brazenly in broad daylight and claims parts of the Word as his own. In John 10:10 Jesus warns us, "The thief comes only to steal and kill and destroy; I have come that they may have life, and have it to the full."

Similar to his tactics to tempt Jesus in the wilderness in Matthew 4:1–11, Satan twists the truth into a well-set trap, cloaked in enticing religiosity.

I can testify the restraints put on me by the teachings that I must earn my salvation, pay back the gift, and fight hard to earn God's favor were all taught from the pulpit, straight from the Bible, and it nearly destroyed me.

To be saved—salvation—is the opposite of destruction.

Run-down; worn out; terrified of life, death, punishment, and pain, the God who died to save me had morphed into a monstrous taskmaster. The cries of worship sounded much more like squalls for help. Common words within the walls of the church broke me. "Well, the devil is after you!" and "God must need you to suffer."

Now I think, *No way*. But then I was too tired to argue.

The Sermon on the Mount is now one of my favorite passages from the Bible. But for a moment, look at it as I used to see it and how you still might. When it is taught that "you have heard it said, thou shall not lust, but I say to you, if you even look at another woman, cut out your eye that you might not sin," and in my terror, I cried, "AMEN!"

Yes, I had missed it. It wasn't possible. And I finally understood that He was clearly saying, "Your way isn't working. I will do it for you. I will do it once and for all, and this gift will be called *Grace*." I was further astonished by this revelation: if the "threats" of the Sermon on the Mount are the way the Church was to run its congregations, we should be passing out eye patches and tourniquets with the grape juice and crackers. But the new covenant teachings after Jesus' death and resurrection do not speak of cutting stuff off; they speak only of new life, hope, blessings, and a grand future.

Greater they say now that it is finished, we can reap the benefits of knowing Him personally, and instead of barely getting by, we can *thrive and rest.*

After I fell into the arms of Grace, I knew the parts of the Bible that were for me, and I recognized the parts that were "for them," those who rejected Jesus and chose to continue to *try* and not mess up. Scripture is profitable for teaching and reproof. Those scriptures are teachable; they are the precursor to the greatest story ever told. What is the lesson? *Jesus*. Again, He was and is the answer. Still, my life was exhausting. Rest evaded me. I knew God wasn't out to get me, but it felt like stress, lack, success, failures, internet trolls, mean girls, and the rest of life's pookie would still be my demise.

I was no longer striving to please Him in that I found great peace. I was in love. My belief in Him and His pleasure in me was my entire truth. But everything else? The basics of life, the day in and day out, well, that left me with stuff on my nose, unable to do a handstand, convinced I was Chinese simply because I liked rice.

I had *just barely* experienced the freedom of His adoration, and still I wanted more. Was this greedy or selfish? Was it too much to ask? Because now in the scriptures, with condemnation behind me, I kept seeing something more.

Ask, believe, receive. . .

Trust, hope, joy, abundance, wisdom, grace, forgiveness. . .patience, and perseverance.

And so, on a late summer afternoon, Justin placed a suitcase in my backseat. I was going away for a week to write my third book. And yes, I would uncover more freedom.

Little did I know I would ask for even more, and He would answer like never before, exactly like He said He would. And it was definitely more, and the unraveling would be nearly too much for me to believe.

But as I poked at the surface and then reached even deeper, I was about to decode things, things that would turn everything upside down and leave me confused, more tired, and more lost than when I started.

Granted, this may seem like the opposite of good news, but He was about to show me things, take me places, and open my eyes to the promises He made and exactly how to experience them. Rest was coming. The real kind. Freedom from want and worry. An inexplicable experience of truly experiencing Him and His easy yoke.

Oh, Friend, we've *just barely* gotten started.

REST, GIRL REFLECTION

It can be upsetting or freeing to learn we are wrong. But I made no progress in my relationship with Jesus until I asked Him to set me free. Once you have tasted freedom, the prison cell is no longer home.

DREAM JOURNALING

Read Matthew 4:1–11. The enemy tempted Jesus. What references did he use from scripture to try and convince Jesus he was speaking with authority?

Chapter Three

THE MIND GAME

Do not conform to the pattern of this world, but be transformed by the renewing of your mind. Then you will be able to test and approve what God's will is—his good, pleasing and perfect will.

Romans 12:2

You just couldn't let the Buddhist ashram launching from chapter one go, could you?

Yes, my third-oldest child, Luke, lived and worked at a Buddhist ashram in Colorado. If you don't know what an ashram is, I will explain. An ashram is a hermitage, monastic community, or another place of religious retreat. A Buddhist ashram celebrates Buddha. Please don't email me about this. I have had my fair share of criticism. I have a blanket response:

Dear Reader:

We do not get to decide what our children become or believe as adults. You can prime them to be something specific, but this is not North Korea. You cannot make them do your will, worship your God, decide who they love, or lock them in the basement. That is called kidnapping. I know because I've had some run-ins with the law.

Jesus be all over you,

Jami

Granted, my run-ins with the law were not for kidnapping, but don't think I didn't look into it.

Among the fatigued women I have encountered, this is of the most significance. We think we know best. We probably do. Still, we do not get to decide many things for our children. It really is not fair. The blood, sweat, and tears of motherhood do not advance us in our control of the beings who called us "Mommy." Basically, as soon as they master walking, we can chase them, but their singular identity and need for us fades with every step.

Ungrateful, nasty, wretched brats.

Luke gave me my parenting wings. Maggie, our oldest daughter, was easy. Well, we thought she was hard, but that's just because we were green. When you've lived in an apartment with your best friends, studied or partied late, and then slept until 3 p.m. the next day, you are a little sleepy, but you are basically rested. If you were to fall in love with your roommate's hottie cousin, get married, and live in a little cottage in the mesquite forest of Texas, you might be worn out from barely making ends meet and working to advance. But there was the weekend, a nap on the couch, toast and coffee on the porch, newlywed rest.

That first baby is like a bucket of ice water to the face.

She is the rude introduction to exhaustion you had not known.

However, looking back, Maggie was a cakewalk. The baby boy that followed, even easier. John slept through the night, never cried, and took six-hour naps. Luke, well, Luke was a whole new level of exhaustion.

But what he lacked in sleep consistency and rage control, he made up for in dimples and compassion. He had this thing about him—from a very young age, he recognized suffering. And as he grew and tested everything we knew about parenting and patience, he was consistent in his love for his friends and an intense desire to save the world, specifically sea turtles.

Luke's best friend since he was five is David. David and Luke met while we were building our dream house on our ranch. David's dad, Joe, and Justin worked together on a lot of projects. So, when Joe came to brick our house, Justin was excited to tell Luke that "Joe the bricker" always brought his son, David, with him to jobs.

David and Luke were instant buddies. For whatever reason, their first meeting is etched in my brain. They stood on the bluff of our ranch, and Justin and Joe helped them shoot soda cans, remnants from the workers' lunch, with their BB guns. They played in the mounds of construction fill dirt and ate peanut butter and jelly sandwiches under an old oak tree. David and Luke were opposite in flesh tone and identical in spirit. They were soft spoken and compassionate, they laughed with and at each other, and they were protective, nearly chivalrous, in their dedication to one another.

In junior high, the duo added a friend to their tribe: Parker. The three were inseparable. David and Parker nicknamed my son Pastor Luke. They knew they could count on him to have their backs.

David's dad, Justin's dear friend "Joe the bricker," passed away when the boys were thirteen. Parker and "Pastor Luke" never left David's side. A few months later, Luke spiraled out of control. To save Luke from himself, we were forced to send him to a military school. I talk more about that hard season in my second book, *Sacred Ground, Sticky Floors*. Luke wrote the afterword to that book. It is one of my greatest treasures.

But during Luke's absence, David and Parker wrote to him. They encouraged him and, most dearly, took care of me. David would text me, HEY MRS. A, HAVE YOU HEARD FROM MY BOY? HOW ARE YOU HOLDING UP? A few times he left notes in my mailbox, telling me he was praying for me and asking to go with us if we went to see Luke. When Luke returned home, the "Squad," as they referred to themselves, fell right back into constant companionship.

Luke started attending Abilene Christian University after graduating early from high school. Parker and David were moving to Austin to go to school. My son, John, had joined the Marines, Maggie was fresh out of college and newly married, my book-writing career was just launching, and Justin and I decided to move to Houston.

With Sophie (our youngest daughter), Sam, and Charlie, we sold the ranch and moved south. At zero hour, Luke asked to come with us. It was here in Houston that Luke started doing yoga. This was the best of Luke. He had a peace about him we had not witnessed. And he decided he wanted to teach. One of his friends was a teacher and had trained at an ashram in Boulder, Colorado. He asked us to help him go and get certified.

He never came back.

That sounded terminal. And to me, in some ways it was. Everything I believed, everything I taught him, was being rejected. But the nickname "Pastor Luke," coined by David and Parker all those years ago, continued to define him. Luke has stamina and work ethic that is hard to match. I knew when he left that the owners of the facility would be dazzled. And not just because Luke is entirely gorgeous, but because he is nothing if not the most committed and faithful worker one could hire—he comes to serve, not be served. He finished his certification, and they asked him to stay on to live and work.

The conscious part of my brain knew this was a good thing for Luke. He needed to be on his own. He needed to work and earn his own money. Luke needed to teach and nurture. He craved the quiet, reflective space of the ashram. And although he was young, he was old enough. I didn't get to decide.

My subconscious was freaking out. Scripture about false gods and the fires of hell tormented me. But again, I didn't get to decide. The choice was his.

Several months after Luke moved there, I had turned in my third book, *Well, Girl*, and Maggie and I decided to visit Luke at the ashram. While writing the book, I had sought freedom from the lie that my body, whether thin or fat, dictated how Jesus loved me. I'd debugged my brain of diet culture, and I was feeling good, a little more rested, and a little bit more progressive in my quest for more of Jesus.

In my research, I watched and read a lot about quantum physics and the mind. It left me in a space of confusion, mostly because I am not a quantum physics kind of girl. But I knew from experience, God had led me to the information. I did not know at the time what He was trying to show me about the magnificent design of the human brain, but I did know He would answer my pleas for wisdom and clarity (see Jeremiah 33:3). I figured it would just take some time.

Maggie and I flew to Denver, and Luke picked us up and took us to the ashram. It was beautiful, and Luke looked fantastic. Eating a strictly vegan diet and meditating for hours a day never made anyone look bad. But there was more. For the first time in his life, Luke looked. . . rested.

The child who cried more than slept, the boy who craved companionship with David and Parker in lieu of food or sleep, the man-baby who never said no to adventure or a party, appeared to be drenched in peace and rest. My subconscious whispered, "It's not real. You can't have that kind of rest without Christianity." My conscious mind said, "I know what I am seeing. He has something. . .something I do not."

Rest.

For four days, Maggie and I did yoga in the mountains with our beloved Pastor Luke. He taught philosophy. Yeah, the child that repeatedly got his head stuck in the Lincoln Log tin taught philosophy classes to retreat attendees. He worked in the kitchen and prepared us and fifty others beautiful meals. He ate with us and then bolted to the kitchen to clean. In remarkable time, we found him at our next yoga class, ready to teach.

Although he appeared to be running full speed on all cylinders, he never looked weary. He was drenched in peace and rest. And this will seem wrong, it is not how a mother should feel, but I was jealous.

When we left him, I wasn't worried or fretful about him. How could I be? Yeah, Buddha not Jesus—you don't have to remind me. But he was safe, healthy, and happy, and I couldn't criticize that or the fact that he was rested and I was not.

I know. You're thinking, you did yoga and took naps for a week? Yes, I napped well. High altitude and low oxygen are excellent for achieving unconsciousness. But my mind was never fully at rest.

Sure, I was free from the striving of "making Jesus love me," because I knew He already did. Period. But I was not free from the stress of life. I would hand my heavy yoke to my Father in heaven and think, "Not my will. . .His." But moments later, another life debacle would occur, and I would think, "Do I hand this over to Him too? Or fix this myself? If I pray and ask for help, will He not help with the other heavy burden? And if He doesn't? What if He doesn't help me and I am supposed to do this hard thing and. . ."

It was relentless. And I was so run down, stressed, and exhausted, I felt like I would break. So, entrenched in this defeatist cycle, I put my computer and cell phone upstairs in a cabinet, terrified that I would wake unable to face the burdens of "Christian leadership," and mindlessly, yet purposely, deleted all my social media accounts and let everyone on my team know. . .I'm done.

If that wasn't bad enough, I slowly slipped into the second entirely real depression of my life. No, not just a little weepy. I found myself driving to the store, and when I came to the bridge over the lake, my mind would whisper, "It would look like an accident. . . . Justin and the kids would be better off without you. All you do is fail."

I stopped driving that route.

The mind games I played with myself were so far off base from the promises of Christ, and some of His promises still felt unattainable. Life and its disappointments kept happening, and I felt a victim to it. All I could think was *If this is all there is to freedom in Christ, I'm moving to the ashram*. Hypocrisy chased me. Please, hear me when I say, I love and believe Jesus. The grandest confusion I experienced in this space was "How do I profess this good God while staying in my pajamas unable to stop crying?" Maybe this is at the core of authenticity. I love Jesus, and sometimes I need a prescription.

In a few months, my third book launched, and I was free of food and body image struggles. That was a miracle in and of itself. Still, I was drowning in a real depression. Looking back, I can say thinking that there will be no psychological or emotional hiccups in this life, with or without Jesus, is like saying, "I am baptized and saved. I never will have to fear a paper cut ever again!"

In a fog of brokenness, I went into Luke's old bedroom and pulled books down off the shelf, and I began to read. I read all of them. The surprise twist? Everything I read began to match the research I had done months earlier while writing *Well, Girl*. Every line I read ignited my subconscious to its scriptural match. Fatigue and the brain fog began to lift.

I was like a mad scientist, which truly makes no sense. If you are a fan of the show *The Big Bang Theory*, you will understand me when I say, I am not a physicist. I am Penny.

I went back to my notes from *Well, Girl*. I watched the videos I had studied just months before, but now I was getting it. Now, stay with me. I'm not trying to mix theologies: the Bible is the truth, and Jesus the Son of God is my friend. Still, there was something in those books and videos that pointed back to something I had overlooked or contrived in scripture. Believe me, I don't think you need to add anything to Jesus to make Him and His teachings truer, but He used something from science and my research to point out something I had missed.

I saw the budding growth of what I was looking for. Greater faith wasn't about willing the mind to believe and receive rest and peace. Greater faith was about changing the mind and then expecting to see and experience God and believing as if you'd received (Mark 11:24). Furthermore, *we can do this.* It is totally possible.

For weeks I continued in my studies. Day after day I saw such peace and freedom. There was a methodology to this; there were answers! I continued in my quest, and I found this space where faith and humanness battled. Jesus said: "Therefore, if anyone is in Christ, the new creation has come: The old has gone, the new is here!" (2 Corinthians 5:17).

More than anything, what I wanted to experience as Grace was exactly what He meant. *Jesus did mean what He said.* And I say this all the time, but it cannot be said enough. There is no *but* in a perfect "I love you." Jesus didn't say, "I love you, but you need to get your act together or else!" No, Jesus said, "I love you, still."

What I was beginning to see was that, yes, you can find rest and peace *when your mind was in line with the words of your mouth.* My mind was the problem. My limiting beliefs and subconscious's incessant chatter were the issues! And while I still had some digging to do, I believed my mind could be made new! Why did I believe this? Well, I had been transformed into a new creature with a new mind when I wrote *Stolen Jesus*. And then I had been set further free when I wrote *Well, Girl*. But, more importantly, I knew it was true because Jesus said so. "Do not conform to the pattern of this world, but be transformed by the renewing of your mind. Then you will be able to test and approve what God's will is—his good, pleasing and perfect will" (Romans 12:2). My fingers flew across my computer.

I knew at that moment this book, the book you are holding, would exist. It would take some time, and I had to have some proof to share. I took a deep breath, the first in a long time, and I quickly recognized, "This is rest."

Believing Him is rest.

Knowing for sure that Jesus is present, that He has

a plan, a plan to prosper, hope and a future (Jeremiah 29:11), was everything.

It was thrilling and intoxicating. On top of that, it was 8:30 p.m. on December 31, 2019! New Year's Eve. I whispered, "Twenty twenty is going to be a year I'll never forget. I have just unlocked the door to rest. . ." and my phone rang. Delighted to see his name on the caller ID, I chirped, "Hey, Lukey! Happy Almost New Year!"

"*Mom. . .*" His voice cracked.

"*David is dead.*"

REST, GIRL REFLECTION

There is no *but* in a perfect "I love you." Jesus didn't say, "I love you, but you need to get your act together or else!" No, Jesus said, "I love you, still."

DREAM JOURNALING

An "I love you, but. . ." is a profession of love with a contingency. It conveys the message "If you don't change or achieve a certain goal, I won't love you anymore." What have you believed you needed to change to experience the love of Jesus?

Chapter Four

OF DEATH AND SPELLING TESTS

There is no fear in love. But perfect love drives out fear, because fear has to do with punishment. The one who fears is not made perfect in love.
1 JOHN 4:18

January 16, 2007

I remember it as if it were yesterday. The vision came to me in the wee hours of dawn, and it came in a flash of perfection. There is no way it was contrived. In the apparition, my beloved Grandma Mickey, who had passed away forty days before this day, and my Grandpa Don, her husband of sixty-one years, were seated by a campfire. I was asleep enough to know I was dreaming, but I was awake enough to be cognizant of every detail. I knew the scenery behind them was at a family-favorite camping spot in Pagosa Springs, Colorado. I recognized the snowcapped mountains and the crisp lake. I also recognized my grandparents. Flannel and denim-clad but much younger, my grandpa poking at the campfire, sucking on a toothpick, and my grandma strumming her guitar.

I watched them intently.

They looked amazing. The mountain backdrop was stunning, with the moon reflecting off the cool, still lake. I was there with them, but they paid no attention to me. I just stood there watching them. They looked so at home, so peaceful.

I was ripped from the vision when my phone vibrated on the nightstand. Through sleepy eyes, I made out a text message from my dad: JAMI JO, GRANDPA DON PASSED AWAY A FEW MINUTES AGO. HIS SUFFERING IS OVER. CALL WHEN YOU ARE UP AND AROUND. I LOVE YOU.

Yes, sometimes death makes sense.

David Anthony Devora was born on October 9, 1999. He was only twenty years old. He, Parker, and David's cousin were watching a football game. They were not in a street fight or out partying on this New Year's Eve. A knock at the door and gunfire are all that Parker remembers.

David was shot multiple times through the door of a little house in a quiet neighborhood near the university. He never even saw the face of his killer. Just as disgusting, his four assailants were even younger than David. The getaway driver was a pregnant eighteen-year-old girl. Five lives destroyed in a random act of violence embraces no lovely dreams or peaceful meaning.

Senseless is not a powerful enough word.

Twenty-seven hours later, I sat in the ghost town–like baggage claim at Houston International Airport. Every time I thought I was out of tears, more would bubble up. I couldn't wait to hug Luke, and yet, I was terrified to see my brokenhearted son. Would he spiral out of control? Would this loss be too much? What if all the hard work of "saving" him crumbled in the wake of gun violence and a precious life lost?

All those thoughts dissolved when I saw his six-foot-three lanky, hippie frame floating down the escalator. He looked tired but peaceful. His dimples flashed, and in an odd turn of events, I collapsed in his arms and wept.

At David's funeral, one priest said, "David would give you the shirt off his back." The pallbearers all snickered and snort-laughed. Later Luke said, "David was a great guy, but he would no sooner take off his shirt for a stranger than participate in a ballet performance of *The Nutcracker*."

David, who had always been as chubby as Luke was skinny, swam in his T-shirt and awkwardly folded his arms to cover his protruding belly. He would help any way he could, but no, he would not be taking off his shirt.

Another priest, David's close friend, told a more plausible story. Days before his murder, David had attended Mass with his family. After the service, David waited for the priest and invited him to breakfast. The priest commented on David's snazzy shoes. David bent to untie them, saying, "Oh here, you can have them." The priest stopped him and said, "David, don't take your shoes off! Those are two sizes too big for me, and you'll be without shoes!"

Two days later, as the priest left his home for the day, he found a brand-new pair of shoes just like David's on his porch with a note from David. He was just that kind of guy. The priest, so devastated by the loss of his friend, was unable to speak any further. The loss was just so unjust, so unbearable. David's oldest brother stepped to the pulpit and finished the tribute.

This story makes me tired.

And this was at the core of my unrest.

From a distance, I watched David's mother with unquenchable curiosity. She seemed good? That evening after the funeral, she asked "the Squad" to spend the night in David's room. She gave some of his things, tokens of David's memory, to each of his friends. They told stories and laughed.

This woman, who had buried her husband just a few years before, now generously hosted man-boys and told story after story about her murdered "bonus baby boy," who delighted her in every way.

Meanwhile, I trembled in terror at the mere thought of such an existence. I was terrorized by the thought of burying a child. And, with Luke home from the ashram, I worried that old patterns would emerge, and all would be lost. Anxiety taunted me. My prayer journal was filled with desperate petitions for Luke's well-being and my own place of peace and rest.

The memory of David was quickly being devoured by the fear of the unknown and the terrors of death.

But I am a believer in Jesus Christ and the promises of heaven?

Yes.

And yet, fear of death hunted me.

I wanted more control than life offered.

I jotted the statement down in my journal.

"I want more control. I want to know that everything is safe and well. I don't want to just constantly pray for peace, I want to experience it. I want to truly believe. Your yoke is easy, Your burden is light. . .and I am worn out."

I resolved to the belief that this was the essence of my faith walk. Ask, *kind of* believe, then buckle up; there is no telling what will happen next, but don't worry, it will be *God's will.*

His terrifying and perfect will.

Eleven months later, I was in a hotel on the beach in Galveston, Texas, pounding out the unfolding that has brought me to rest. What I must say first, above all else, is this—bad things happen, and Jesus is not the author of tragedy. Amid grief and fear, a worldwide pandemic, and political and civil unrest, I met with rest.

The pain of earthly death is not forgotten. The gut-wrenching memories and stories we can all testify to are not minuscule. And no, I have not buried a child. If you have, let me just say. . .*I am so sorry.*

There is this thing that happens among believers in Christ, this verbiage about how the deceased loved one is in a better place and their suffering is over. I suppose that is of some solace. But it neglects the cold, hard truth: those who are left behind are left to cope without their beloved. The knowledge of this pain is fuel for the brain, and it can obsess over this simply because it's not what you want. You don't want to feel the pain of loss.

I remember the funeral of a dear friend at the ripe old age of forty-three. At the time, I was thirty, and I may have considered her "middle-aged." Now at forty-nine, I am certain she wasn't. As her husband and young son stood at the podium thanking everyone for loving them well, her beloved man said, "*We were having so much fun. Yes, that's it. . . . We were having fun just being together.*"

Eighteen months before that, shock and concern assaulted me when I met her in the vestibule of the church, and I begged, "Helen? Were you in an accident?" She, with a fantastic British accent, said, "Bloody hell! I have no idea what is going on! A week ago I woke up unable to feel my damn leg!" I ducked twice as she let loose "bad words" in the house of the Lord and cursed the walker that barely helped her inside.

As I watched her "men" agonize through the salubrious goodbye, I recounted her continued rapid decline and ultimately untimely death from ALS. Many "bad words" flooded my pounding head. Praise be to God my throat was restricted with grief, or I'd have blurted them out right there in the church, which may have resulted in an exorcism.

And I am going to say something, a thing Christians shouldn't say. Death is a tragedy.

Certainly, I believe in the eternal glory of heaven, but it doesn't overrule the decree down here of being "dead." And dead hurts the living, yes, even the Christian living. There are the common clichés, ones that deserve a "Would you please shut up?" While others warrant a punch in the throat. Heed the warning. Yes, I am suggesting a movement, a nonpunishable assault for throat punching a funeral attendee who says, *"God must've needed another angel."*

Throat punch.

There are the sincerest condolences, genuine and dear. But when I think of those left behind, I'd beg to argue the injustice. *"We were having so much fun. Yes, that's it. . . . We were having fun just being together."*

Death most rudely interrupts life. Its intrusion leaves enormous gaps in normal. It invades every emotion with the intensity of memory and summons a solitary space, a space that will never ever be the same. A most intimate place, where no matter the tender familiarity, no one knows "exactly how you feel."

Yes, the Christian species is blessed with the hope of heaven. Still, the trouble with a dead Christian is they are still dead. Eternally made whole, still gone, still not here with us—where we most enjoyed their company. *And we were having so much fun, just being together.*

Recently, a friend of mine's dad passed away. Her words, "I am simply heartbroken," sum up everything about being left behind. And I relayed the death to a mutual friend, and I said, "He was only sixty-seven." A few weeks ago, another acquaintance passed, and I lamented a more advanced age with the same mystery. "He was only eighty-nine."

I remember as a child cowering under my sheets, secretly weeping, heartbroken over my daddy's birthday party that evening. I couldn't bear the thought of him growing older, and the candles on his cake had brought me to radical distress. At the time I believed that after this milestone birthday, he wouldn't have much time left here on earth.

He was thirty.

Forty-plus years later, my dad continues to delight in life. Age is relative in death. Death still means someone you enjoy is no longer joyful of company. Their age may inflate the injustice, but that person is still dead. And truly, this stinks. There isn't any other way to say it. Well, there is, but then this chapter would just be another "Chin up, see you on the other side! Jesus loves you! Let's have some potato salad!" composition.

I did not mean for this chapter to morph into a "dead stinks" manifesto, but I'd like to recommend that God is big enough to handle the fury that naturally accompanies "dead." And this is a testament to rest.

I imagine Martha, who by the way is my favorite biblical character, storming from the house, "Bloody hell, Jesus!?! He's dead! Where have you been? Our brother is dead. And we were having so much fun. Yes, that's it. . . . We were having fun—just being together. . ."

And what did Jesus do?

He wept (John 11:35).

This baffles me more than death. He knew what He was going to do. Jesus was about to raise Lazarus from the dead. Moreover, He is JESUS. So, He above all others "should" have been like, "It's cool, Martha. We will see him on the other side. Chin up. Do you have any potato salad?"

Ah yes, how we "should" behave.

Right.

If Jesus can raise a guy four days out and still weep

at the tragedy, there's no surefire "should" in dead etiquette.

I have been surrounded by peace in seasons of loss. But I've also nearly drowned in the wrath of grief, and for this I always felt guilty. I used to believe that the pain of grief would be my undoing. A lot of this belief stemmed from things I had been told about how I should feel about death.

Death is not as awful for Christians because of our hope in Jesus.

Don't cry or make a scene; look strong.

You should be over this now because of Jesus.

You should be happy they are no longer suffering and are with Jesus.

I have come to know two things about grief. One is, just because a Christian or a fellow churchgoer says something doesn't make it true. And if a trespass stifled you or made you feel your grief was not warranted or understood by your Father in heaven, He didn't inflict the wound, a human did. That human is just as prone to folly as you are. So don't blame Jesus.

Second, grief is a celebration, a carnival of loss. It is a loss worth celebrating, worth remembering. Grief is the cost of having loved well, and the right to mourn that love, and the absence of it. This mind shift has been a welcome gift in the area of rest. The loss of a loved one is a treacherous path, but I've come to understand that it's possible to experience loss and not lose our peace. We can hold both tightly in our grip and still be the unique and peaceable individuals we were created to be.

Over the last few years, our family has faced loss.

We have grieved well, and now, with a newfound understanding of how our minds work and our God, we have simultaneously mourned and rejoiced. This is rest.

Furthermore, as creatures created in the image of our Creator, He fashioned the emotions associated with death. He wept at the loss of life, fully cognizant of what waited for Lazarus on the other side. I submit He did this because death stinks. It is all the things that mess with a good life. Truly, it is the most basic antonym to living.

Death means that part, the piece of life we were enjoying so much, is no more; and if that makes you furious, you were fashioned by someone who created fury. He created laughter, tears, mourning, and dancing. He is not shocked or offended by the deep belly cries of the living while grieving the dead. In the self-righteousness of our salvation, we have shoved a "Do Not Mourn" sign down the throats of the heartbroken. Among the helpful and wise, we have told them what they should do instead of letting the grief chips fall where they may. Yes, we have the hope of eternity, but that hope does not mean we are prohibited from grieving.

Death rudely interrupts life. Healthy Christian platitudes don't change the hurt of being here when someone you adored is not here. And I am not saying you should, but I am most certainly not saying you shouldn't, untuck your shirt, kick off your high heels, let loose the controlled bun pinned nicely atop your weary head, and let it rip. Kick wide the door to all the feels: happy memories, awful ones, the loss, the hope, the injustice, and the grace. Fling wide the deep gut wails of "dead stinks," and recognize the nonsense of life without someone you adored.

For as great as we have loved, wouldn't it make perfect sense to mourn with the same intensity? I propose that God gave us all these feels. Mourning isn't a sign of a lack of faith. I find it of great comfort to know I will meet my loved ones again on the other side, but that is of no consequence to the fact a dead Christian is still dead. Alive eternally with the Lord? Yes. Bless. Those of us down here? Jesus, help us.

So, to kick off this new season of rest, I simply encourage the brokenhearted: rage on. Here among the shattered and wrecked, you are most cared for, you are seen and known. Rest in your grief. Be held. Instead of questioning this good God, deciphering His will, rest in His comfort.

The memory of the pangs of death and the fear of it are essential parts of unrest. I will expand on this exponentially, but for now, I will start here. There are only two choices from this page forward: love and fear. Love is the greatest commandment (Matthew 22:34–40). This is easy to remember. Love is the solution by which all things make sense and all living is made easy. It cannot be neglected or denied.

Fear, on the other hand, is born of past experiences, our own or ones we have been witness to. Fear is the great thief of rest. Fear is multiplied in the mind out of habit. My friend, fellow author Carey Scott, calls this "circling the mountain."

It is the essence of worry. A mind that repeatedly goes round and round, playing out the unknowns and working through worst-case scenarios, is a mind that is not at rest. And the mind is a powerful companion. It replays that which we wish to forget, and moments later it refuses to remember where you left your car keys.

The mind feeds off memories, and when it is not satisfied with those images, it makes up the unfathomable and holds it as truth. Have you ever awakened from a dream, your heart pounding, drenched in sweat? That is because the mind cannot comprehend reality from the vision. The body responds to dreams and visions as if you have really experienced them.

How can we stop this? Well, we can't. And we don't really want to because this is the job of the mind, to keep us alive and safe. I would like to suggest that part of the fatigue so many Christians experience is based on memory and a mind that won't let go of that which is not for us (1 Corinthians 10:23). It is bogged down with terrors of death, taxes, and all things hard. Nestled deep in our beliefs is the ongoing banter of the world, platitudes, and beliefs about how we "should" feel. And if you say something enough, visualize it often, that terror is what your brain considers truth. It becomes your belief.

The good news is you can undo these lies. You needn't walk away from memories that you hold dear or that keep you safe. But the promises of Christ, an easy yoke, a restful friendship, are true. The bitter tastes I had associated with how I should behave made way for new beliefs that He intended for us to rest in.

I am a dyslexic author. The greatest invention in my lifetime is spell-check. Aside from that blessing, the thing that has been paramount in my ability to learn and succeed has been association. I associate best using memory pegs. Colors, pictures, stories, or jiggy rhymes have always been a huge help to me in remembering things that my bouncy brain has no real interest in re-counting. Among those little cues, the one that is now a trophy in my display case is a third-grade spelling test, one that I failed twice.

I sat in a small office, the fluorescent light overhead glitching in a way that only further distracted me. The teacher's aide sat across from me and warmly encouraged, "You can do this." Obviously, I believed her to be wrong. We went over the words ten more times. The threat of being held back, which would not happen for another two years, meant nothing to me. At that moment, I just wanted to be done. But I was helpless to escape elementary school and even more helpless to escape the little room and the impossible list before me.

She continued, "Let's look at this word one more time. Believe."

I picked up my pencil and with much frustration and discouragement wrote *B-E-L-I-V-E.* She shook her head. "No, sweetie. It is B-E-L-I-E-V-E." Tears filled my eyes as I stuttered, "I don't understand. The *e* makes the *i* long?" She smiled and nodded. "Very good. But this time it is different."

Of course it is.

"This time there is an extra *e*. It is BE-*LIE*-VE. This will help you. Always remember this: there is a LIE in everything you BELIEVE." I don't remember whatever happened with that test, but I have never spelled *believe* wrong since. Greater, I have since seen this truth: there were a lot of lies in everything I believed, especially in my faith walk as a believer in Jesus Christ. Furthermore, I believe there is a wealth of lies we believe about Christ that offer no rest. I can't pretend to know you, but I will be so bold as to say, if you are here, you share in those fallacies and want a way out. I believe freedom and rest are what you want, and Jesus will answer.

In Matthew 14:25–26, Jesus walks on water through the rough sea. Frightened, Peter says, "If it is you Lord, invite me out to you." Jesus invites Peter out onto the water, and Peter is able to walk on the water. And then what? Well, Peter remembers that he can't walk on water. Consciously, Peter knows that Jesus said he could, so he does. And then his subconscious, or his heart, what he knows to be real, reminds him, "Dude, you are just a man. Man cannot walk on water." And Peter begins to sink.

Peter's love for Jesus gave Him the ability to walk on water. Peter's fear of drowning was what sunk him. His fear, the deep TRUTH his subconscious knew to be the facts from his experience as a fisherman, overruled his profession of love.

If you are sinking in unrest, if you are baffled as to why the miraculous evades you, if peace is overridden by fear, and your prayers appear to go unheard, could it be because your real prayers, the prayers of your heart and beliefs, are not in line with the words of your mouth?

What I have discovered is that, while we need to know of the dangers of oncoming traffic, rest comes when we feed the mind a different scenario: not the worst-case scenario but the option of a best-case scenario.

In the meantime, grieve as you loved—fiercely. And if anyone tells you how to behave in the wake of your memories, you can punch them in the throat. I will bail you out.

REST, GIRL REFLECTION

We have the hope of eternity. That hope does not mean we are prohibited from grief.

DREAM JOURNALING

Do you harbor any fears that you now realize were not instilled in you by God? Do you have a story of "church hurt"? Write it out in your journal; get it out of your head and onto paper. Tell your mind where that B-E-L-I-E-F originated.

Chapter Five

SOUR GRAPES

Finally, brothers and sisters, whatever is true, whatever is noble, whatever is right, whatever is pure, whatever is lovely, whatever is admirable—if anything is excellent or praiseworthy—think about such things.

PHILIPPIANS 4:8

What perfect timing. As I compose this chapter, it is election day 2020. I put up a social media post this morning, and one comment led perfectly into this chapter. I meant no harm. It was just a snapshot of my little red convertible, top down, with the Gulf of Mexico dancing in the background. As expected by my readers, it was just a comical tale of my folly upon arriving in Galveston Island to write. Imagine my shock when I was brutalized by a reader.

How could I be so shallow? The fate of the nation is in play. The comment was angry and laced with contempt for my lack of concern over Republican or Democrat.

Actually, I don't know why I am shocked, except that it came from a close relative. Unfortunately, this is the state of our society—angry, primed, and ready for a fight.

I am not here to enrage or provoke you. I am here to talk about rest. And I sound much braver than I am. When this book hits shelves, it will have been six years since I met with my first online assault, and many more would follow. Still, they hurt my feelings. I try not to look at the comments, but it is a privilege to be in the position of author and teacher. My morning emails and social media posts are nearly always the result of some time alone with my Jesus and the revelation that follows. The interaction with readers is dear to me. If I don't read the comments, I cannot respond. And I want to respond. . .well, to the kind ones.

I ignore the hate to the best of my ability. It does not define me. At the same time, I confess, one thing that is wholly true of me is, I really do care what people think of me. I am not sure there are many of us who don't.

My friend Susannah B. Lewis, author of the foreword to this book, is hilarious. With over a million followers on social media, Susannah's audience gets doses of hilarity and raw observations and opinions that leave many in stitches and others primed and ready to pounce.

If I have had one conversation with Susannah where we have vowed to "never post again," I have had fifty. The fact is, even if you are southern, bold, and sassy, being told off is a yucky feeling. From behind their iPhones and laptops, hateful humans say things to other humans that would rarely be spoken in person. Repeatedly I am asked why I don't get political on my pages. And while I am confident in my response, I still limp a little when venom is tossed back.

I don't get political on my pages because I am a teacher and speaker of freedom. I am not here to tell you who to vote for. I am not responsible for how you arrived at your convictions, but I do believe that those convictions matter. What I want for humanity is rest. . . real, tangible rest. If I make an observation about the love of God without a partisan manifesto and later I tell you a ridiculous story about Sam and Charlie, it is simply what I love to do. Love turns work into rest.

I love my work. Rarely, if ever, do I feel the angst of "having to work." I mean, I write from the depths of joy and freedom. When I am not writing, I paint daisies. *I get paid to paint!*

Parenting two little boys at my age is comical. Can there not be a space on the expansive web where one can go and just cut loose, experience biblical insights, and have an occasional good laugh? Well, I would like to think yes. And then I remember a post from months ago. I wrote a post about a conversation I had with our six-year-old Charlie.

Charlie asked me, "Mommy, can boys become ballerinas?" I answered him, pretty sure my little linebacker had no hope of ever dancing the flight of the butterfly, "Yes, boys can become ballerinas." He pondered this and said, "Oh, gosh. I hope that doesn't ever happen to me!"

A simple exchange, comprising maybe fifty words, words I thought were hilarious, between me and my little boy turned into a brutal battle in the comments. The first was the accusation that I was a homophobe, and the next was a ruthless attack on my lack of compassion for homeless African American transgender teens. I still can't make heads or tails of either. The rest were attacks on the attackers. Y'all, I appreciate you coming to my defense, but this is a waste of rest. You cannot negotiate with terrorists and. . .brace yourself. . . Facebook doesn't define the truth of who we are.

On one of Susannah's and my manifesto calls where we resolved to delete our social accounts and return to a life of simple motherhood and serene farm life, the conclusion was made, this is a ministry. Social media in all its folly has some blessings. And I do have peace and rest, but I can promise, you won't find me trolling the pages of Instagram looking to be hot and bothered or enraged.

Are you looking for a fight? Worse, are you expecting one?

Those questions are for me as much as they are for you. I send out an email nearly every morning of the week with a mini devotional for the day. I invite readers to respond to the emails with prayer requests. Keep in mind, to receive my emails, which I admit are exponential in delivery, one must click a button, fill out an online form, agree to the terms and conditions, and possibly prove they are human and not a robot. Subscribers must make a choice to receive my emails. No one is forcing them to do this.

So, when someone responds, one would assume it is someone who wants to read what I wrote and needs prayer or wants a healthy dialogue about the content. Why then, when I receive those responses, does my heart race and I peek out of one eye before reading, fully expecting an attack? *I have taught myself to be afraid of comments.* The email responses are sweet and dear 99 percent of the time. They are encouraging and tender. But I have made it a practice to expect to be sucker punched.

This is not rest. This is stress.

If you have ever had food poisoning from a bad batch of chili, eating chili is never the same. Chili may have been your favorite; if you are ever able to swallow another bite, you do so with great caution. This is the protective power of memory. It is instilled in us from birth. Even a sleeping newborn will dream of suckling; that is what he or she knows from memory. Peacefully sleeping, a baby's little rosebud lips will softly bounce as if they were indulging in warm, life-giving milk.

By the same token, a child that has been physically abused will duck and cover when someone raises a hand around them. Our memories are a collection of life-giving habits and life-saving routines. At one point in our foster care journey, a little girl we were caring for was eating lunch in her high chair. I had methodically cut her grapes into hundredths to protect her from choking. She loved grapes. But on this occasion, she began to spit and scream.

Upon further investigation, I found out that the grapes were not ripe enough and had a pungent, sour taste. And that was it for the picky eater and grapes. She would run from the dining room if there were even plastic, decorative grapes on the table. Her love for the taste that once delighted and nourished her had been replaced with one bad experience. And just like that, all grapes were bad.

Scripture tells us in Philippians 4:8, "Whatever is true, whatever is noble, whatever is right, whatever is pure, whatever is lovely, whatever is admirable—if anything is excellent or praiseworthy—think about such things."

What are you thinking about that has you so stressed and consumed that you found yourself here, in search of peace and rest? If it is grocery money, car troubles, illness, or the looming death of a loved one, worry is something that strikes us and leaves us physically and emotionally run-down.

There are many things in our lives more pressing than others. And while we do need to be informed about our world, we don't have to drown in its hopelessness. I cringe when I hear the opening sound bite for morning news channels. It is altogether too much. And what is the truth?

If nothing else, the COVID-19 pandemic has given us all plenty to talk about, at a distance of course, *sometimes*. Personally, I have had to make decisions that were based solely on instinct—the "unbiased" media has been of no help to me in my quest to not get Covid. I am no expert, but you are reading my fourth book. My entire writing career was launched five years ago by telling my kids they weren't that great and writing thirty-one blog posts on stuff I wish you'd quit saying.

This has been a mixed bag. For one thing, I have found I too am not that great, and for another, trolls. If you don't understand what a troll is, allow me to tell you, because that I understand. If nothing else, maybe you will conclude "Oh my gosh! I am a troll!" A troll is a person who reads random posts or *everything* on social media and then adds their unsolicited opinion to either

1. Appear wise.
2. Be a jerk.

As I said, I have been around just long enough to know that I shouldn't read the comments; but like the rest of society, there are some things I just don't understand. And I am a hard study. Sometimes, I go into my closet and cry. When I do get a hateful email or comment, it is almost always by someone who met with one line of commonality within a post that had nothing to do with the entirety of the post and took offense. Society doesn't seem to read all the way to the bottom. They seem to enjoy being offended, or the trolls outnumber the common folks.

The other thing that a good portion of society doesn't understand is that we are being watched. Our data is being collected. I've had the problematic job of explaining how Google ads work to several of my readers. At least twice a week, I get a message from a reader that starts with: "Hi Jami, I'm a huge fan. . .but I am so offended by the ads you run on your blog." Often this is an easy but awkward response. Those are Google ads, and they are based on your search history. But sometimes, like this week, I just don't respond. I feel like there is no appropriate response to *"I am never reading anything you write again! You say you love Jesus and then an ad on your blog is advertising girl-on-girl dating sites! You should be ashamed of yourself! Using the facade of the risen Lord to promote the homosexual agenda is an abomination!"*

Truly, I cannot babysit all my readers minus one as of this week. I have been misunderstood before. But before you tell me off, you might want to check yourself and make sure you aren't telling on you or someone in your household. I am not using Jesus for financial gain, and Google knows what you like. . .and all your secrets. Now, so do I.

I consider Jesus a good friend. He blessed me with six "not so great" children, which affords me plenty of material. And He lets me see things others might miss. The Lord does provide. For instance, the guy at the grocery store this week, unloading his haul of toilet paper into his truck. Others walked right past him. But I saw him. He had a surgical mask on. That isn't an unusual sight these days. But this rocket scientist had a slit cut in his mask, where a lit cigarette dangled. Also, I meant no offense to rocket scientists.

I really wanted to stop and ask the masked smoker a few things. First, it was a paper mask. I feel like this was a face fire hazard. Second, you know, the mask is to cover the mouth to prevent the spread of the virus? So, when you cut a hole in the front of it so you can nurse on that cigarette, the germs are not contained. Finally, I kind of feel like you have bigger health issues looming than the coronavirus. I have spied a lot of folks who don't understand the face mask concept. I think this guy was their leader.

And yes, I understand, that will be offensive.

But! I am not a troll. So, I didn't ask or offer my

opinion to the masked smoker. I just saved the information in my writer's brain, thanked the Jesus I am not using for my financial gain with ads for girl-on-girl action for providing more content, and went inside to get milk and bread. . .and more toilet paper.

This is where I witnessed more things we as a society don't understand—life basics. There are simple things, like the line that says twenty items or less. Ma'am, either you cannot count or read or. . .you are just super arrogant. And sir, that Def Leppard 1987 Winter Concert Tour T-shirt simply doesn't fit you anymore. It's over. You have received your full due for the payment of that big hair band memorabilia. Your fifty-plus-year-old-man beer belly is disparaging to everyone who ever loved the band.

I don't just witness "bad" things. I have a keen eye for seeing compassion. I saw a boy tell his mother he was going to help an elderly woman take her groceries out to the car. The dear gesture reminded me of something my man-babies would do. So, I took a beat and cried in aisle seventeen, where I also threw an inappropriate supply of Cheez-Its into my grocery cart.

Something else society doesn't understand: Cheez-Its are essential.

With all the confusion and misunderstandings already in place, I simply must ask you, what are you inundated with? What provokes you? What pushes your buttons or pushes you over the edge? We all have our triggers. I am glad that this chapter was composed before the election was called. Of course, I have an opinion. I mean, *obviously*, I have an opinion.

But my opinions don't all have to be in line with your opinions. And whether we like it or not, whether you agree with me or your blood boils at my suggestions, we are one. We are the body of Christ. And when we polarize the body, it is ineffective. If you woke up this morning and your right arm left you a note that said, "I no longer am going to be your right arm. I am going to be the Scout troop den mother Sarah's right arm," you would be facing a long day.

Rest assured, that was not a jab at lefties! Good grief, so easily offended.

You see, we have these convictions, and we arrived at them for a reason. Even if they are "wrong," our Father in heaven sees His children as beloved. He sees Christ in you. Second Corinthians 2:15 tells us "we are to God the pleasing aroma of Christ." This is simply precious. Imagine sinking your face into the soft black curls of a newborn baby and inhaling deeply that new human smell. Don't like babies? Imagine puppy breath or the smell of your grandma's turkey casserole.

The point is, we are the pleasing aroma of Christ to God. While I will talk much more about the freedom of forgiveness in the second section, it is important to note early on: forgiveness brings rest. It is not always easy to say the words. Honestly, you may not even mean them when you say them. But "I forgive you" is paramount in our quest for peace.

Scripture tells us, "As he thinketh in his heart, so is he" (Proverbs 23:7 KJV). Now, here is the trouble we all encounter. We aren't the problem? Outside forces add to our trouble. I am not the one who leaves my smelly socks on the coffee table. And what about the rest of the population? Personally, other humans cause so many of my worries.

This is going to be hard to digest. So, hear me out.

It is not them.

It is you.

Let me finish.

That thorn in your side? They can literally be the nastiest human on the planet. You are responsible for how you are impacted by everyone outside yourself. They may have robbed, cheated, stolen, or violated you. Hear me when I say, I have been a victim of both physical and emotional trespasses. And I am not responsible for someone else's violation of me, but I am responsible for my response.

This dictates what I watch on television. Okay, you got me. I am a fan of reality crime television. But I am not going to bury a body in my backyard, because that is not for me. And this has been of huge help to me. It isn't that you cannot watch the news all day long or tell people off on Facebook. You can do that. Nothing can separate you from the love of Jesus (Romans 8:38–39). Everything is permissible, but is it beneficial (1 Corinthians 10:23)?

Is the media you are feeding your mind a benefit to you? Is the relationship that leaves you stressed and physically sick worth it? Are you focusing on what is good, pure, and holy (Philippians 4:8)? Are you feeding at the slop trough of despair and misery or basking in the peace and rest of the banquet hall?

We are invited to be whole, healed, rested. It is only

when the world and its brokenness sound louder than the gentle voice of Jesus that we chose to toss and turn in unrest. That is on you and me. So let us not blame Jesus. He bought our ticket out of the madness.

REST, GIRL REFLECTION

There are many things in our lives more pressing than others. And while we do need to be informed about our world, we don't have to drown in its hopelessness.

DREAM JOURNALING

Is there someone or something that is causing you unrest? What can you do to change this? Is it a radical removal from someone in your life? Or do you just need to turn off the television? Talk to Jesus about this, and then in the quiet, listen for His tender answer.

Chapter Six

WHAT IF. . .WOW!

We demolish arguments and every pretension that sets itself up against the knowledge of God, and we take captive every thought to make it obedient to Christ.
2 CORINTHIANS 10:5

It took me a long time to arrive at this place, because I didn't speak the truth of a lighthearted human. This became most obvious right before I launched my "I am" cards, which I was doing with my young sons. Charlie, our youngest, was struggling with keeping his hands to himself at school. A note came home from the principal that said, "Charlie has no self-control."

I was offended because that is not the totality of who Charlie is. I mean, he's potty trained. He doesn't run through the house screaming. He has table manners. He has some self-control; he just was struggling in this area. And in the past, when grappling with one of our older sons, Luke, we had spoken the opposite of his struggle to him when trying to correct him. "You are not a delinquent. You are set apart and chosen as good."

I'll get back to the relevance of that, but first I want to talk about an important concept. As believers in Jesus, we were promised a few things when we accepted the gift of salvation. Peace was one of the things promised. I am now going to introduce you to some more concepts to get you quickly seated in the lap of a worry-free, restful life so you can move from anguished stress to joyful bliss. And the most important concept to address is your mind: the playing field of worry and the seat of unrest.

We are going to look at the conscious mind and the subconscious mind. Hang with me. This is a golden key to unlocking a life of true rest. The conscious mind is the part of the mind that is taking in this information. It is the part that said, "*Yes, I want to find a way to stop the madness of constant unrest.*" The subconscious mind is the stubborn little bugger that whispers, "*No! Let's not do anything new,*" and "*Hey, what if this doesn't work? You have tried it all before!*"

Now, don't worry about what the subconscious is saying right now. It is both friend and foe. The subconscious mind runs on experience, reality, and perceived reality (i.e., the imagination). The conscious mind operates on the information you feed it, experiences, and memory. For me, the best example of this is the desire to start getting up an hour earlier to go work out. The conscious mind lays out your workout clothes, packs a gym bag, puts a bottle of water in the pocket, and sets your alarm for an hour earlier than usual.

When the alarm goes off, the subconscious mind

is the part of the mind that hits the snooze button and starts the banter. *"Stay in bed, we will work out tonight after the kids go to bed or next week."* If you follow that lead, later the subconscious will remind you, *"I knew you wouldn't do it. You never stick to your commitments."* So, while the subconscious keeps you safe and reminds you about the consequences of a hot stove or to yawn or eat lunch, it also is the breeder of much worry and stress. It is the master of limiting beliefs. It is also what can be dubbed the mother of self-sabotage.

Here is a sturdy example: There are layoffs at your place of employment, so you decide (with your conscious mind) that you are not going to fall into the trap of worry. Instead, you are going to trust God with mountain-moving faith. You put a Post-It note on your computer that says *"I can do all things through Christ. Philippians 4:13."*

You keep your nose down and chant this as you watch the guy next to you pack his cubicle and use his pink slip to blow his nose. The subconscious goes to work based on the information it is witnessing, experiencing, and remembering. It feeds the conscious mind messages like "That guy got laid off. He's been here longer than you! He secured the Patterson deal. If they got rid of him. . .you're next!"

You keep chanting under your breath, *"I can do all things. . ."* And the subconscious argues, *"No you can't! You need this job! What are we going to do!? Do something! Stop reciting scripture and do something!"* So, even though you have not received your walking papers, you start googling new jobs, still chanting, but allowing the subconscious to defy your conscious mind's decision to have faith and do all things through Christ.

Whether you are laid off or not, later the subconscious mind will remind you, "*Wow, you have so little faith. I thought you said you were going to be more faithful.*" If you did get laid off, it might say, "*Wow, you of little faith, of course, your prayers aren't answered.*" If you didn't get laid off, it might say, "*Wow, you of little faith, all that worrying for nothing.*" Either way, you stress over how little faith you have, welcoming unrest.

Now, don't be mad at the subconscious. Its job is to keep your reality in check. And this is tremendous. The subconscious mind is turbocharged on feelings. If it hasn't seen it, felt it, heard it, or experienced it, it will not want you to go outside of that reality. With your conscious mind, you say you believe that God is your refuge, and the subconscious mind reminds you of every bad thing you should avoid from its experience.

Last time there were layoffs, you were out of work for three months.

Your car was repossessed.

You just barely paid off your credit card.

And the stress builds. There is a chemical response in your body, adrenaline releases. Your heart is pounding, maybe you are sweating, and your mind races with memories of a past struggle or one you witnessed someone else go through.

Then the subconscious mind says, "*Geez, you're a wreck! I thought you had better faith than this. Pastor Matthew told you that your faith should carry you through anything and to trust in the Lord. Why won't you calm down?*" Little monster.

But here is the good news!

You can change the subconscious to work in alignment with the prayers and intentions of the conscious mind. I am not just saying this—nor is it a figment of my imagination—Jesus said it too. Romans 12:2 reads: "Do not conform to the pattern of this world, but be transformed by the renewing of your mind." The issue is, we have been working on the conscious mind to overcome doubt, worry, and limiting beliefs. With our conscious mind, we say, "*I am not going to worry or fret. I trust Jesus. I have the mind of Christ, and I will not be forsaken.*"

The subconscious mind says, "*MMMMM-k, you know you have four kids to feed? Do you know how to turn one box of macaroni and cheese into three boxes? No? I didn't think so.*" And the cycle continues.

However, by identifying the separation of the conscious and the subconscious "voices," and by using the conscious mind to add new data to the subconscious mind, we can renew our minds and live in the most fun, lighthearted, restful mind space ever. This is the essence of rest. The first step has already been taken. Your conscious mind is now privy to the subconscious mind's tricks. Now we are going to start taking it and its narrow thinking captive with the "What If Wow" method.

Currently, worry and stress are fostered by the subconscious game of "What If Ugh." The subconscious is feeding you worst-case scenarios. That is all it knows to do. Its job is to keep you in the familiar. In this life, bad stuff happens all around us. The subconscious is sending the What If Ugh messages and kicking the dog out of our faith.

What if you get called back next?

What if you must get a job far away with a longer commute?

What if you can't buy your daughter a new bike for her birthday?

What if you can't buy your daughter a new bike for her birthday, and she is so fraught with disappointment, she starts seeking comfort from random boys and gets pregnant and you're a grandma at thirty-six, and then she goes to prison for shoplifting and you have to raise the baby!

How are you going to raise a baby?! You can't afford diapers?! You don't have a job?! What if you have to steal apple juice for the baby? What if you end up in prison for shoplifting too?

Five seconds later, the subconscious says, "*Wow, what if your faith was better, maybe none of this would have happened. . .*" Yeah, thanks, subconscious. But we are going to retrain the subconscious by playing a new game, one that has entirely changed my life. I call it the "What If Wow!" game. The What If Wow game is the new volley to the subconscious's What If Ugh game.

So, the subconscious says: "*What if you get laid off?*" And instead of succumbing to that line of thinking, we banter back, "*What if I get a promotion?*" or "*What if I get laid off and get a huge severance bonus, and I can go back to school?*"

While your subconscious might be saying, "*What if this lady is a soggy fruit loop,*" tell your subconscious the soggy fruit loop said, "*What if I am, but I can help your human finally rest and trust?*" We aren't only going to take every thought captive, we are also going to feed it fresh food by following the specific instructions from Jesus in Philippians 4:8: "Whatever is true, whatever is noble, whatever is right, whatever is pure, whatever is lovely, whatever is admirable—if anything is excellent or praiseworthy—think about such things."

What If Wow is just that—instead of entertaining negative, scary, or limiting beliefs, we are going to focus on the good stuff. Now, there are some people this is naturally easy for; they are probably not here. They don't read books on how to not worry and rest. But I want to tell you a story about a non-worry kind of guy, my Marine son, John. John is now twenty-three years old. I spent a lot of years worrying about John. As a child, he struggled with learning disabilities, and I thought he would never have a "normal life."

When John was five, we got him a puppy. John named the puppy Bosco. Bosco was tiny, less than a pound. And frankly, Bosco was kind of weird looking. Bosco was the product of a breeder's mistake. The breeder had a Pekingese purebred business. The breeder's husband had a purebred rat terrier. One day the rat terrier and one of the Pekingese mamas had an. . .encounter. The canine couple produced one female Pekingese rat terrier. They decided to keep her. A couple of years later, that Pekingese rat terrier got out and met up with a basset hound. A few months later, the Pekingese rat terrier gave birth to two male puppies. . .Bosco and his brother, Rosco. Yes, Bosco is a Pekingese rat terrier basset hound.

On our first visit to the vet, John handed Bosco to the doctor, and the vet took one look at him and said, "What is it?" And I said, "A Pekingese rat terrier basset hound." The vet did the examination and then said, "John, I need to talk to your mom. Could you take Bosco and go wait in the office?"

The pet doc informed me that Bosco was not a healthy puppy. He explained that he would have problems eating because his jaw was deformed. Furthermore, Bosco probably wouldn't live more than a year. He was bowlegged, had double vision, and *if* he made it past one year, he would experience terrible joint issues. I knew John would be heartbroken.

On the drive home, I told John the hard facts, and John said, "What if that isn't true? What if the vet is wrong? What if he lives for thirty years? What if he is just fine?"

Yes, what if?

Like I said, John is now twenty-three. Bosco is eighteen, which is roughly calculated into ninety-eight in dog years. Yeah, ninety-eight. Bosco is an old man. He's a little crotchety. He is mostly gray, blind, and walks with a limp. He naps a lot and has wicked bad breath. Recently, I asked John, "What if Bosco needs to be put down while you are deployed?" And John said, "What if he doesn't? He isn't in any pain. He still eats and goes for walks. What if he lives another ten years? What if he wins the world record for the oldest and ugliest living dog and he's finally famous? What if someday he just peacefully falls asleep after a long and happy life?"

Indeed.

This is worry-free, restful living. It is faithful and trusting living. John's mind looks for positives, and because of that, he witnesses miracles. Miracles are not sighted as often by worriers.

Why, you might ask? I will tell you why.

The subconscious has a partner in crime. It is called the RAS, or the reticular activating system. The subconscious mind is the part of your mind that holds deep beliefs, habits, and your "go-go data." The RAS is like the gatekeeper of the mind. It is a small group of cells at the base of your brain stem. It filters the incoming "data" or images, tastes, sounds, colors, textures—not smell, but all your other senses. Our brains can only process so much of this data at a time, so the RAS decides what is important to you and what is not.

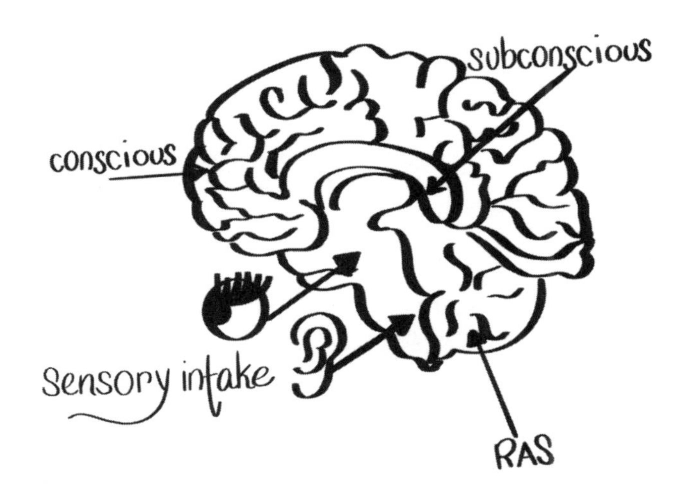

How does it do this?

Well, it responds to what you focus on most within the subconscious or your deep beliefs. With millions of thoughts and data being thrown at you, the RAS filters out what is not your focus.

I like to use a car as an example. Have you ever noticed when you are driving on a busy highway with hundreds of other cars that you most readily spy a car exactly like yours or someone you care about? You spot those vehicles quickly while the other cars just whiz past. Those cars are not important to you—they are of no relevance, and if you had to notice every single car on the road, you would most likely lose your mind. But if a car exactly like yours speeds past, the RAS lets that image through the gate because "HEY! We have that car!"

When I bought a bright red convertible Volkswagen Beetle, I ran by my parents' house a couple of weeks later, and my dad said, "I see red convertible Volkswagen Beetles everywhere I go! I never noticed them before. Now I see them constantly!"

My dad drives a jeep and a Harley. Convertible Beetles meant nothing to him prior to my purchase. After I bought my Beetle, my dad's RAS allowed sightings of them because I AM IMPORTANT TO MY DAD. His RAS filters in the little red cars because they have relevance to him now.

So, if you are constantly worrying and entertaining "What If Ugh" statements, the RAS lets the negatives into the subconscious to play. Now imagine you are working at your desk and you're completely lost in a project. You've heard rumors of layoffs, and you have been reciting worst-case scenarios. Out of the corner of your eye, you see a coworker headed to the boss's office.

Normally, immersed in your work, you might not have noticed that any of your coworkers were walking to the watercooler, let alone to the boss's office. But the RAS sees everything, and it filtered the movement to the subconscious as a red alert. With layoffs looming, the subconscious goes into action. "Uh-oh, what if Cameron is about to get laid off?!"

You start your chant, "I can do all things through Christ. . ." But here is a new option, "What if Cameron is getting that promotion? What if she moves to that new department? What if I then get her job? The one I have wanted forever!"

Then, you flat-out pray that prayer, believing as if you have received (Mark 11:24) and *feel* all the good feelings of having what you want! "God, I pray right now in Jesus' name for Cameron's career. I know she really deserves that promotion. You know I would love to be in her current job. I am totally qualified, and I would be really good at it. I love You and I trust You, either way. I can do all things through You! Amen."

At first, while you are retraining your mind, you will have a little struggle. The subconscious might say, "Promotion!?! Are you a madwoman? They are laying people off!" But you can retort with "I serve a God of miracles! The sky's the limit!" Then, to further your beliefs, you draw the subconscious into submission through "I am" statements.

I encourage you to say them into a mirror not as a mystical mantra but so the RAS sees you and hears you and knows the information is of validity to you. The RAS will then let the information through to the subconscious, and you will begin the process of lighthearted living effortlessly.

I am loved and protected.

I am confident.

I am trusting.

I am peaceful.

Yes, I get it. Let's say you *did* get laid off? Okay, same principles. The What If Ugh scenarios start barking:

What if you must get a job farther away and must start commuting?

What if you get to spend less time with your kids?

What if you can't buy your daughter a new bike for her birthday?

Take those thoughts captive with the What If Wow and positive I am statements:

What if this is the way I move on to something closer to home?

What if my new job pays more?

What if I get to spend more time at home?

I am given great opportunities.

I am creative! What if I get to be more creative at my new job?

I am trusting! What if this is the answer to prayer?

I am seen and known! And God knows I am ready for a new challenge! WOW!

The more you do this, the more the subconscious knows "This is how we do it!" And it will become more comfortable with this lifestyle of peace and rest than a lifestyle of worry and doubt! Voilà!

That said, your subconscious is who you say it is. If you say, "I am a worrier," the RAS filters worrisome data to the subconscious, and the conscious, which is trying not to worry, now has the incessant internal battle of worrying about worrying. This was my conviction: if I am a believer in Jesus Christ, I am a new creation. The old has gone. The new has come (2 Corinthians 5:17)! If I continue to live in worry, stress, and doubt, my subconscious is not in step with my conscious, and I am not at rest. My conscious mind can spout scripture all day long. My subconscious may even have them memorized, but until I *feel* and experience new data, the subconscious is going to demand I stay in the same "comfort zone" of what it knows.

I am only new when the subconscious agrees, "Yep, things are different!" "I am" statements* are so powerful because they tell the subconscious how things are, not just how you wish they were or might be if you got your act together. Then the subconscious, whose job it is to keep you grounded in reality, will start looking for proof to show you *"Yes! You are those things!"*

**Just to be clear, we are not calling ourselves the great I AM, but we are agreeing with what God says is true of us—those whom He calls His own.*

Again and again I will remind you, "As he thinketh in his heart, so is he" (Proverbs 23:7 KJV). This was huge to me. I cannot experience rest if I am thinking or saying the opposite! If I am constantly professing my impending demise, talking about what a horrible sinner I am, and complaining about how hard I have it, I am speaking against who Christ says I am.

Furthermore, Jesus did not die so that we could "kind of" be saved. If you are drowning in the ocean and I throw you a life jacket, you might be able to tread water. But a shark might come up and attack you from below. Or a storm might come, and the waves might rip the jacket from you. If instead, I come in a boat and take you safely back to shore, drive you miles from the ocean, and buy you lunch, you are saved. You are not going to drown in the ocean at this time.

Jesus did not die so that you might be saved with a "but." He loved you so much, even while you sinned, He died so that you might have life abundant. All the promises He made with that sacrifice were meant to be ours. Not kind of ours or just barely ours, but all ours. You are bought and paid for (1 Corinthians 6:20).

The fruits of the Spirit are not something we are supposed to *try* and accomplish (Galatians 5:22–23). An apple tree doesn't *try* and grow apples, it just does. That is its nature. Our nature as the *saved* is constantly sabotaged by the beliefs our subconscious experienced prior to the revelation. You can say you believe in the death and resurrection of Jesus, but the subconscious has never experienced or witnessed someone being brutally murdered and then rising from the dead three days later. So, while it is trained in the faith, it is your doubting Thomas or sinking Peter. It craves some proof.

If any of that were true and this guy was raised from

the dead so that you might live where there is love, joy, peace, forbearance, kindness, goodness, faithfulness, gentleness, and self-control, why don't you experience them? Well, if you have believed those are yours to achieve, not a gift or your very nature, they are evading you—again, no rest.

Oh, but this is complex when we are not privy to how the mind works! The subconscious is the battering ram that is robbing us of rest. And now, you know what it is up to. This is where the rubber meets the road. Yes, you can sit and meditate for hours on rainbows and butterflies, but until your subconscious sees some evidence of how you want to experience life, it is going to want to stay in the realm of worry and stress because that is what it knows and understands. It is going to give you more reasons to worry because its job is to help you make sense of the world around you and keep you alive. If it believes that you live and breathe fueled by the negative, that is what you will continue to experience. This is exhausting, no?

Yes. Yes, it is. And there is much more to taste and see.

REST, GIRL REFLECTION

It is possible to take every thought captive with "I am" statements and a clear understanding of parts of the brain that have been allowed to work against your faith.

DREAM JOURNALING

What negative statements do you make on the regular that you can turn into "What If Wow" statements?

Chapter Seven

OH, HUMANITY

He created them male and female and blessed them.
And he named them "Mankind" when they were created.
GENESIS 5:2

I used to fight with my mother-in-law in my head until I made myself physically sick. I would let these maddening scenarios play out to the point my heart would be racing and I'd be hysterical. I expected the worst from her. And what did I get? The worst of both of us.

I am blessed to have remedied that. Her last months on this earth were spent in my care, and I am eternally grateful for that time in service to her and my husband. However, if I had been privy to What If Wow, instead of being fueled by What if Ugh, well, I imagine there would have been a lot more peace in our lives.

I remember driving to take one of my babies to my mother-in-law's years ago. The entire way to her house, I rehashed the last time we had seen each other. Even though apologies were made, I expected something awful, and that is what was created.

In a situation like this, where the mind is running on memory instead of love, I was thinking:

What if she says I look fat. . .then I am going to say. . .

What if she asks why the baby hasn't had a bath. . .then I am going to say. . .

This is a worrisome and stressful mindset. It is not good, pure, holy, or lovely.

What If Wow would have been driven by expecting the best, like this:

What if she says I look great. . .and then we have a lovely conversation about the new aerobics classes I am teaching.

What if she says can I bathe the baby for you? Then I can cry on her shoulder about the heavy load of graduate classes I am taking.

I can almost guess what you are thinking. "But then I am not prepared for an attack?" Okay, let me retort with this, "Are you ever *really* ready for an attack?" When you arrive at a location where you may or may not be attacked, are you dressed in the armor of God when you are drenched in sweat and ready to vomit? Or are you more approachable, confident, and at ease when you have been drenched in whatever is good, pure, and holy?

At the risk of sounding cliché, *what would Jesus do*?

We have these lines memorized, we know who He was, and yet the battle between what we are saying with our mouths and believing in the subconscious is leaving us entirely defeated with worry, stress, and unrest. And, oh goodness, it is so tiresome. Jesus told us, "Come to me, all you who are weary and burdened, and I will give you rest. Take my yoke upon you and learn from me, for I am gentle and humble in heart, and you will find rest for your souls. For my yoke is easy and my burden is light" (Matthew 11:28–30).

This is who we are in Christ, but if we speak the opposite, the subconscious knows how to respond only to what it is experiencing. What I missed for years was that by saying scriptures over and over without experiencing any of the truths, except in random chance encounters I called "God things," there was no evidence to truly be wholly changed!

Now, what about the impossible person you must encounter? Say your mother-in-law makes mine look like Mary Poppins? I have two recommendations. For those whom you absolutely cannot escape, be it a relative, an ex-spouse you share joint custody with, your boss, or pesky neighbor, entertaining the What If Wow habit is an effective catalyst to rest. Expect better by speaking better. Expect better by planning for a wow instead of an ugh. Focus on whatever is good, pure, holy, and lovely; and be drenched in Jesus and know because your subconscious is trained to *know* better is possible.

No, you cannot control someone else, but you can choose your response. Does this mean you don't get your feelings hurt or there isn't a brawl? No. But it does mean you have the upper hand because you are expecting the mountain to move and your subconscious fully believes that can happen because, in cooperation with God's original design, you have trained it to expect and see good things.

The impossible person that doesn't have to be in your life? They don't get to be around you. That is how you become responsible and find rest. It might be awkward, and it might be hurtful and hard, but you get to decide. I recently made two decisions like this. My prayer for those humans, whom Jesus loves and died for, is "Go, be made well away from me."

I wish them no harm. I pray they find peace and rest. But when I found myself worrying when their name came up on the caller ID or I received an email or text from them, my wow moment was "What if I didn't have to feel this way anymore? What if I didn't have to be sad or upset? What if the removal of these relationships that continually defeated and hurt me made room for new, better, and healthier relationships?" And that was it.

There wasn't a fight or an argument. I just stopped answering. Eventually, I went so far as to block them. I stand by this. If someone is truly hurting you, they don't get to have the privilege of being in your life. *They don't get to be around you.* They are responsible for how they decipher that information. You are responsible for you. You are responsible for how you feel, and if you feel bad in their midst, you get to decide that you are not going to have that in your life anymore.

Please also know that sometimes God asks us to do hard things. But if He is asking you to do it, there should be some peace in that space. You can trust Him to guide and protect you. If you have asked Him to do this and you are seeing changes or are inspired in how to help the person and yourself, then that is every reason to stay. Above all, stop, get still, and ask Him. Don't worry about how He will answer. He is not the nagging voice of the subconscious. He is the instant first voice of calm.

One aspect of unrest I felt for too long was that if I ended a relationship that was toxic to me, I had not been a "good Christian." But this is the most empowering truth: that person or persons has a Savior. He died so that they might live. I am just a girl. I have a loving family, a full-time career, and a ministry I adore. I wasn't the sacrificial lamb; He took care of that. He knew I wasn't capable of such a feat.

And here is another What If Wow: What if by ending that relationship, Jesus will lead them to freedom and peace that they have not known? What if He has someone who can help them as soon as you are not their punching bag anymore? What if their whole life is made better when you are not the focus of their abuse anymore?

This is also very important—a person who is toxic to you only gets to have more authority in your life than God *if you believe they have that authority*. Again, that is on you and me. If we believe a promotion at a job, a custody battle, or any other thing is more in the hands of a human than the God who loves us, we are shackled to limited belief. We are robbed of rest and steeped in worry if we entertain the thought "They rule my future."

Recently, an acquaintance called me in hysterics. Her ex-husband, who had abandoned her and her three small children over four years ago, had filed for custody of her children. Her ex was very wealthy and had hired a high-profile lawyer. Her lawyer was fine, but his specialty was in real estate. Granted, the ex-husband had several cards stacked against him. He had not visited the children but on a couple of occasions, and he was behind in child support. His reasoning for filing was arbitrary at best. Still, it was scary.

My acquaintance was inconsolable, but I suggested the What If Wow game. She would spend the next month imagining the best-case scenario instead of the worst. She was reluctant, but she had nothing to lose. She had no other options. So, if she had the thought "What if he wins custody," she would say out loud, "What if he doesn't?"

Then she would let her imagination run wild.

What if he terminated his rights?

What if he pays his back child support?

What if he leaves us alone from now on?

The morning court arrived, and we spoke briefly. She was a little nervous, but she was doing surprisingly well. I waited for her call. When she called, I could barely understand her. She was screaming, "He did not show up!" He didn't even show up. The judge dismissed the appeal and demanded that the ex-husband pay for the court costs.

A few weeks later, I asked her why he hadn't shown up. She said, "I have no idea. We haven't heard from him. But my lawyer said that because of the filing, his failure to pay child support was recorded as well as his recent huge pay increase. He paid the court costs, and because he was wanting to move out of state, he was forced to pay the back child support or his wages would be garnished. The child-support payments were increased, and so far they have been on time." What seemed like the worst-case scenario turned out to be the best-case scenario.

Sure, you could argue that may have happened even if she had been submerged in worry. And it may have. But would you rather take a nap in Hawaii or the back alley of a sewage containment facility? When something is completely out of your control, entertaining the worst-case scenario is torture. Entertaining the best-case scenario is faith.

Scripture tells us: "Can any one of you by worrying add a single hour to your life?" (Matthew 6:27). Now, I know some of this may still seem too good to be true. I would argue, Jesus is too good to be true, but I believe with all my heart that He is exactly who He said He is.

When we are steeped in worry and unrest, when He said we didn't have to be, we are only believing with our conscious mind instead of changing the subconscious to take our beliefs to the depths of our understanding.

Changing my mind about outside forces that threatened my rest was the key to what I had been missing. However, the mind actually speaks in imagery. I am going to show you an image, and you will see what I mean. What does this sign convey?

That's right. It's universally understood that this is a sign for a men's and women's restroom. Even if you are in a non-English-speaking foreign country, if you see a sign like this, you can assume a restroom is near.

I remember a story a pastor once told. A little boy and his family moved to a new school that was inside a Catholic church. His math scores at his previous school had been very low, mostly Ds. When he began coming home with straight As, his parents were curious about the drastic, positive change. They asked him, "Is your new math teacher really good?" The little boy replied, "She is really scary! She has a plus sign over the door with a dead guy nailed to it! I am working really hard so that doesn't happen to me!"

As Christ-following adults, we know the image of a man nailed to the cross is a Crucifix, not a method to advance a child into fearfully memorizing their math facts. Although, sometimes it takes whatever it takes. But imagery is how we are also able to convey a message to the subconscious and notify the RAS the image means something to us. In the previous chapter, I told you about my dad spying red convertible Beetles. I had sent him a picture of the car. On the day I got the car, I drove by his house and showed him the car once.

A couple weeks later, he told me he saw them everywhere. My car is adorable, but like I said, not only is my dad not a Volkswagen guy, but also he would have to fold himself in half to drive the car. He's too tall to have an interest in the itty-bitty vehicle. So, it only took him knowing "My daughter drives a car that looks like this" for his RAS to start filtering those cars into his line of vision. The convertibles became important to him because of love.

He doesn't care about the car image, but he cares about the Jami in the car image. He wants to see me any chance he gets. And because that is life-giving to him, the RAS tells the subconscious, "Hey! There's your girl!"

What else can the RAS do?

Well, if love inspires peace and rest, imagine what images that you hate do? This is the essence of watching a scary movie through your fingers. If you choose to sit down and watch a horror flick, and you know you won't be able to unsee it, you cover your eyes. You know yourself well enough to know *This is terrifying! I don't want to relive this.*

But the RAS perceives your raised heart rate and terror. Once you see it and respond through *feeling*, it will remind the subconscious "There it is again!" The subconscious clings to these things because it now knows a clown with a bloody machete is something to look out for. Even though that image is your greatest terror and you hate to see it, the mind is now looking for this horrible thing to protect you and keep you on alert.

Now imagine a person you dislike greatly. If you think about that person and then you rehash the past or daydream of your next encounter, you are feeding the RAS and subconscious a hearty serving of What If Ugh scenarios associated with that human. The stress of those images encourages the RAS to be on the lookout for the person and people with similar dissatisfying qualities. Essentially, it feels like everywhere you go, you are reminded of this toxic person. And yes, you are because the subconscious wants to keep you privy to that which is "bad" for you. The subconscious cannot decipher between emotions; it just knows that the body responded to the image.

When I was in the first grade, a little girl from a neighboring school was kidnapped by a man in a white van. We were taken to an assembly at my elementary school and shown pictures of what the van possibly looked like. For the next year, while waiting for the bus, we would all scream and scatter if a white van drove past. To this day, even though I drove a white van myself, the sight of a white van alerted me to danger.

In all fairness, I would like to think my mind knew that I was too cool to be driving a twelve-passenger van.

The old adage "What you resist persists" can be wholly attributed to the RAS and subconscious. What you resist is what you are imagining over and over again. When you are focused on hate and fear, you are tormented by hate and fear. When you are focused on whatever is good, pure, and holy, you are finally at rest. When you are running ugliness through the mind nonstop, there is no peaceful resolution. You are again circling the mountain with survival hypotheticals. When you are fueled by love, you are buzzing down the highway on cruise control. This mind space is the spirit of rest.

Of course, there are some things we need to remember as "bad." It was smart to tell five hundred elementary schoolchildren to be on the lookout for a predator in a white van. It allowed us to be cognizant of danger. However, when we continually group humanity into categories of bad guys, we are again separating ourselves from love. Friend, love is not only the greatest commandment, it is the totality of our identity in Jesus. He is love. And He created us and dwells in us. This is who we are. Until we say it and B-E-L-I-E-V-E it, it is who we are not.

Again I say to you, "As a man thinketh. . ."

My friend who went through a brutal divorce was in a Facebook group called something along the lines of "Man-Haters." The stories within the group were intense, sometimes comical. The group offered my friend an outlet and camaraderie for her frustrations and hurt after the gut-wrenching split from her ex. But one day at lunch she said, "I hate men. They are pigs." I understood where she was coming from. I can't understand the depths of her hurt because I have not experienced infidelity in my marriage or the carnage of an ugly split. But I had to remind her, not all men are pigs. My friend wanted to start dating and hoped to eventually remarry. But by saying such things about the male species, she was telling the mind the opposite. This is the truth: God created men, and He doesn't make mistakes.

We were given free will. I am not the boss of my friend or you. Still, by "hating men," we are in fact creating a global crisis of nuclear proportions. We are breeding a legacy of masculinity that devours our femininity. We are denying who we are to fight who they are when, in reality, we are more powerful, more essential, more the body of Christ when we raise up "woman" and join forces with man to bring about balance and love. And love is everything.

Jesus told us to love our enemies (Matthew 5:44). He showed us how as He hung on the old, rugged cross. When Jesus spoke the words, "Father, please forgive them, they know not what they do," did the nails through His hands or the spikes of the thorns stop hurting? I doubt it. But did He choose love instead of hate? Yes. And then what? That's right—it was (and is) finished.

REST, GIRL REFLECTION

What we resist persists. What we embrace has the power to do the same. We are invited to rest by changing our minds. This God, His ways are perfect.

DREAM JOURNALING

Do you have a hateful or negative blanket statement you regularly make that you need to take captive? Is there someone in your life that needs to be made well away from you?

Chapter Eight

THE DEEP END

That which was from the beginning, which we have heard, which we have seen with our eyes, which we have looked at and our hands have touched— this we proclaim concerning the Word of life.

1 John 1:1

The harsh realities of life are the focus of the battleground. The fact of the matter is, if someone has hurt us or we are unable to make ends meet, this is what we see and know to be the truth. Our minds are primed and ready for a famine, and the feast that Jesus has prepared before us, well, that seems a little naive. But naivete is what we're called to. In Matthew 18:3, Jesus tells us, "Truly I tell you, unless you change and become like little children, you will never enter the kingdom of heaven."

Welcome to playtime.

Illusion is your new best friend.

When my three oldest children were still at home, they participated in a local swim team. All three of them were actually pretty good. Maggie is built like me—tall, strong, busty, with birthing hips, and just enough "junk in her trunk" to have looked quite womanly at the ripe old age of twelve. John and Luke are built like my dad. They are long and lean. But John, in particular, was also very muscular.

During swim team warm-ups, my brood would stretch on the deck and then put their goggles and swim caps on. They would dive off the block into the pool to loosen and warm their muscles for three hours of lap swimming and technique coaching. Well, everyone but John.

John would jump into the pool holding his swim cap and goggles and sink like a stone to the bottom of the pool. Once at the bottom, twelve feet deep, John would stand on the bottom of the pool, flat-footed, and adjust his cap and goggles. He didn't have to try and stay at the bottom of the pool. He had to kick back up to the top to grab some oxygen and let the water out of his goggles. His 7 percent body fat frame worked with gravity, even under water.

Maggie was determined to do the same. She would jump in the pool and kick and flail in an effort to stand at the bottom of the pool like her "little" brother, John. Bless her. Dear one, breast tissue is lighter than water. You can blame me; she was homeschooled. But no matter how I explained it, Maggie would not vacate her dream of standing on the bottom of the pool.

Baby girl, we float. This is our reality. This is why

more women survived the *Titanic*. We have buoys. We do not sink like stones; we float like Styrofoam cups. Eventually, the flailing scene and the exchange from a training bra to C cups became too much of a battle for Maggie to entertain.

I'm not here to burst your bubble but to tell you to blow a bigger bubble. Miracles can and do happen. Reality is an obstacle to rest. I believe in a virgin birth. And you can't talk me out of my stance on the crucifixion and resurrection of Jesus.

Water walking? Yes.

Healing the sick, suffering, and blind? Oh yeah.

Raising humans from the dead? Yup.

Water to wine? Feeding the five thousand? Mountain moving? You betcha.

Peace, joy, abundance, and on earth as it is in heaven?

Long pause. . .uh. . .well? I mean, it would be easier to believe if only I could see it. Throw us a bone, Jesus. How can we see these things here and now? Why aren't they more rampant? We have professed our love. We have never missed a Sunday. Faith as teeny tiny as a mustard seed, we have that. Why don't we have rest?

And His answer? Because you expect to see unrest.

You believe with your mouth not your heart (i.e., you believe with your conscious mind, not your subconscious mind). Deep inside of us, we know the harsh realities. We have seen and experienced too much. We have felt the pangs of unanswered prayer, and we have quieted our rejoicing so as not to offend those who did not receive a healing or a pay raise.

Who are we to boldly profess miracles in the wake

of suffering? And yeah, I totally get it. We don't want to sound prideful or hurt others. At the same time, if we do not testify to His glory, how will we fish for men?

And so, the battle rages on. Our subconscious continues to look for worst-case scenarios and silences the Good News by spying harsh realities and shushing us, begging us not to make a scene. Oh, but we are tired. Tired of mediocrity and tired of the yes/no/maybe scenarios of our lukewarm faith.

Jesus said, "Truly I say to you, whoever says to this mountain, 'Be taken up and cast into the sea,' and *does not doubt in his heart*, but believes that what he says is going to happen, it will be granted him" (Mark 11:23 NASB 1995, emphasis added).

All the church folks say, "Amen!"

The subconscious says, "Well, I mean. . .I guess. Sure, we could move that mountain, or we could use Google Maps and just drive around it. That is probably safer than displacing a geological land mass. Let's just look for a more sensible route." And we look down at our phones, type in our destination, and miss the rumbling power of God, who was just aching to pick up a mountain and toss it into the sea simply because He loves you and you asked. Bummer, that would have been a sight to see.

Throughout His time on earth, Jesus asked for what He needed. He believed in His heart the truth of who He was, who His Father in heaven is, and it was provided to Him. He could have said, "Go get me a stallion or camel to ride into town." He opted for a donkey, and what did He get? Yep, exactly what He asked for (Matthew 21:7).

Continually, Jesus showed us that His needs were met.

"Draw me some water" (John 4:7).

And it was drawn.

"Be still!" (Mark 4:39).

And the storm subsided.

"Get up and walk" (John 5:8).

And off the cripple wandered.

"Be healed" (Mark 5:34).

Again, health was restored.

"Lazarus, rise" (John 11:43).

And moments later a dead man was having some lunch.

I am most convinced that our stinking habits—beliefs that are steeped in reality—are exactly what keeps us shackled to unrest. In turn, we are not free to be the hands and feet of Jesus. I am positive that was never the intent. The belief that a harsh reality is bigger and more powerful than God, this is the hallmark of exhausted and stressed.

It is hard to comprehend blessing the nations if you can't meet your basic needs and are gripped in terror. Yes, you can pray or donate your time, and this is good, but what would you do if you were unshackled from worry and want? Complacency to a life of lack, or worse, the justification that we are called to it, is the work of the world that uses our minds and the very Word of God to perpetuate the lie that "well, God's will must be for me to be miserable."

Nope.

God's will was Jesus, and Jesus came to give us life abundant. The gamut had been run to try hard and get harder. In the Old Testament, they ran about sacrificing sheep, wandering in the desert, trying to fix themselves and make peace with God. The only answer was, and is, Jesus. He was the perfect solution to the biggest problem: separation from God. God blessed and blesses. That is His nature.

If you found favor with God, like Moses, David, Abraham, and many others, and landed in the pages of the Bible, you were not starving in the streets. Your cup was overflowing! *And that favor was bought for you in the sacrifice of Jesus. All that He has is yours.*

Christ in you, the greatest mystery, the hope of glory (Colossians 1:27).

Again, I am going to encourage you to look at what you are saying versus the actual deep belief of your heart. I am going to do this with Jesus' own words, words He had in His heart and experienced here on earth. What is the difference?

Read the following out loud (Matthew 6:9–10):

"Our Father in heaven,

hallowed be your name,

your kingdom come,

your will be done,

on earth as it is in heaven. . ."

You know the rest. Let's get hung up on that last line: *ON EARTH AS IT IS IN HEAVEN.* Friend, what is going on in heaven? Are there maxed-out Kohl's cards? Is there a lack of puff pastries? Are your overdraft fees greater than your income? If this is the case, I understand a hesitancy in praying "on earth as it is in heaven." I'd opt out of that petition too.

Are we to assume we are trudging through the world only to meet our Maker and hear Him say, "Well done, good and faithful one. Here is a roll of quarters for the laundromat. Machine #12 has a funky smell, and I am not responsible for items that are lost or stolen. Also, the bathroom isn't working. You'll have to cross the streets of gold, just past the pearly gate, and use the lavatory at Burger King."

I think not.

What I have come to experience is that we are caught in cyclical spiritual defeat, which is nurtured and fed by the deep beliefs of our heart (subconscious). So, there are layoffs at our place of employment. This is hard and discouraging. But instead of *believing*, trusting that God has plans for us, hope, and a future (Jeremiah 29:11), and a better opportunity is coming, we back the malady of fear and negativity and settle for less than heaven on earth.

At random, something good happens, and we call it a "God thing." At the next juncture, something bad happens, and we call it an attack from the enemy, thereby giving power to the enemy.

At the risk of sounding bossy, STOP IT.

The enemy gets NONE of my accolades. None. He is a worthless piece of burnt toast. That is all I even want to say about him. Jesus, the Alpha and Omega, Beginning and End, is the One who gets all the credit. Jesus is not even capable of authoring badness. He is love. And "love is patient, love is kind. It does not envy, it does not boast, it is not proud. It does not dishonor others, it is not self-seeking, it is not easily angered, it keeps no record of wrongs. Love does not delight in evil but rejoices with the truth. It always protects, always trusts, always hopes, always perseveres. Love never fails" (1 Corinthians 13).

Love never fails.

Jesus never fails.

And if Christ dwells in us, the hope of glory, the greatest mystery, guess who else will not fail?

That's right.

You will not sink.

You may have been at the bottom; you may still be there. You may have absolutely nothing, or maybe you've given up. And Christ in you will not leave you, forsake you, betray you, or destroy you. You may be starting from zero, completely depleted of hope or even a nap. It might not make a lick of sense—neither does a virgin birth, resurrection, or water walking; still, I believe those things happened.

And now, anything is possible.

Step out on the water. Don't look down. Do not rationalize. Gravity doesn't apply here. Physics doesn't have anything on the Son of Man.

This is what is asked of you:

Do you believe?

I pray you said YES. If you didn't, that's okay. It's hard to get there when reality has been less than heaven on earth. Embedded in us, deep in our subconscious, are things that take action to overcome.

But there's Good News. Jesus overcame the world.

So, now what? Well, first, you have made a huge stride by notifying the conscious mind that you know what the subconscious mind, your deep beliefs, are doing to your relationship with rest. For example, for a long time I prayed for more success in my writing career. I would ask friends to pray about it, and I would write in my journal "PLEASE, GOD! Let my books be more successful!" But the truth was, deep down I was afraid of this prayer being answered.

As I uncovered more and more about my fear and love, I discovered my fear of success. As I mentioned, I struggled in grade school. On top of that struggle, we moved all the time. I was accustomed to being lonely and left out. When I first experienced success in my writing career, the first few days of my first viral post were thrilling. And then came the trolls.

My life was threatened, I got seething emails, people wrote ugly posts and articles about me. It was stressful and upsetting. I didn't want this kind of thing to continue. Then, with no experience of any kind in the world of writing and publishing, I faced a whole new kind of discomfort: other authors pretending to be my friends to advance themselves and a variety of betrayals that still turn my stomach. Couple that with vivid memories of sitting alone at the lunch table, longing for companionship at yet another new school, and you get a glimpse of what my heart was really crying out for.

> *"In Jesus' name, let my book stay on a dusty shelf somewhere, so I will not be attacked or hurt anymore."*

My first book, *Stolen Jesus*, is the story of how I encountered the message of Grace. I look back on how I became published, what I thought I wanted, and what I hoped would come from that experience. That little book is candid. *Stolen Jesus* is a vulnerable look at all the ways I was in bondage to law and trying to make Jesus work the way I understood Him.

But it isn't always easy to be candid. Many people have been impacted by that book. It has invited them to fall into the arms of the real Jesus, who, by the way, is just wonderful. I think I did want it to do well. I just wasn't prepared to be attacked. I am not a confrontational person. I don't like to be singled out. And the fruit of that was a lack of success, for my own protection. When I realized that I was afraid of my books being successful, that deep within me I was afraid of cyberbullies and exposure, I was able to begin the process of changing my mind. What I prayed with my mouth became the prayer of my heart.

Which brings me back to sinking Peter. In Matthew 14:22–33, Peter was invited by Jesus out onto the water. Peter had seen Jesus perform miracles. He actually hung out with Jesus, broke bread with Him—they were good buddies. Peter professed his belief, dropped his net, and actively followed Jesus. I am sure you have heard it said, "Peter sank because he took his eyes off of Jesus." I have always believed this to be the truth. But scripture doesn't actually say that; it says when Peter *felt* the wind and waves he began to sink.

When Peter felt the wind and the waves, his RAS notified the subconscious, "Our human is about to die." Peter's lifetime of experience with the sea demolished the profession of his conscience. Fear of death by drowning was greater than the love he professed with his mouth. Bless his heart, Peter wanted to believe. He walked away from his career, and Jesus was right in front of him continually doing the impossible.

Still, he sank.

So, what chance do we have? We were not at the crucifixion or resurrection. We tell the stories of the miraculous. We profess our belief in water walking, but like Peter, we have no experience with it. We are fully aware of the dangers of getting out of a boat in the middle of the storming sea. And unless you are going to send me a video of you walking on water, I am going to bet that, no matter how much you profess a belief in Jesus, you are going to have footage only of you sinking.

Armed with this new insight, I, Jami Jo Amerine, who hates choppy water and is prone to seasickness, boldly climb out of the boat and step onto the raging sea. I will not look down. I also won't read the comments. I am headed straight into the arms of the Jesus who raises people from the dead and turns water into wine.

Now I boldly pray: "Jesus, thank You for setting me free. Thank You for allowing me an opportunity to write, speak, and teach. It is with much thanksgiving and trust that I hand my books, my career, and my beliefs over to You. I thank You that You are most careful with me. I trust You to do things that no eye has seen, no ear has heard. You be Jesus, I will be Jami, Your beloved. Amen."

And I will follow that up with this: I believe and expect great things.

I know this is what He intended, because I have

experienced it: *He is committed to the miracle.* That is just who He is, the Savior who died so that we might live in the abundance of peace and rest. I am so convicted of this; we say we believe in this miraculous God, but we stop short of believing He will move in miraculous ways, and we miss out on the inheritance that is ours.

We have been invited out onto the water; we just keep remembering how human we are. It's our minds and teachings we have embraced that keep us sinking. This is why we aren't walking in the abundance of rest, blessing the nations, and living a life of tranquility without apology, because we are ignoring the inheritance. We are bought and paid for. Grace is the answer because our sin against God was a debt against Him we could not pay on our own, so Jesus did. The blood worked, and there is nothing left to do but believe.

Look at you! Standing flat-footed at the bottom of the pool.

Next stop, the Olympics.

REST, GIRL REFLECTION

Step out on the water. Don't look down. Do not rationalize. Gravity doesn't apply here. Physics doesn't have anything on the Son of Man.

DREAM JOURNALING

Who does Jesus say you are? What "I am" statements can you add to your vocabulary to instill the fullness of God's power into the reality that is this world?

Part Two

DREAMY

Chapter Nine

HIPPIE CHICK

Behold, I am doing a new thing. . . do you not perceive it?
ISAIAH 43:19 ESV

Back at the ashram, the peace and rest I witnessed in my son Luke, also known in my other books, blog, and social media handles as "the Hippie Baby," was what first stirred my questions. How come he is so at ease? What does he have that I don't? I love Jesus. Why am I struggling so much?

I know if you are committed to Christ, you have the same questions. One could make the accusation that it is all just a show. But I know Luke. And even at the depths of his grief over the loss of David, he was at rest.

This brings us back to 8:30 on New Year's Eve of 2019, before that tragic call about David. The information I had uncovered has brought me through a wretched year *rested*. My profession—"2020 is going to be a year I'll never forget. I have just unlocked the door to rest. . ."—was true. In the days that followed, as we grieved, Justin and I made the conscious decision to change our minds, our subconscious, for real.

We still grieved. And we grieved well. Like the rest of the world, we definitely met with struggle and frustration in 2020, but things were different. I had uncovered the source of my faith walk's struggles—my mind. There were four parts to the "undoing."

1. There is no "but" in a good "I love you." Jesus said what He meant and He meant what He said. He loves me. He came to give me rest. No buts.

2. There are only two choices in life: love and fear. Love produces every good thing in life. Fear produces every negative action and reaction.

3. As a man thinketh, so he is. If I say with my mouth "I believe," but in my heart (or subconscious) I believe my life is falling apart, I am going to fall apart.

4. Christ in me, the greatest mystery, the hope of glory (Colossians 1:27) means I am consumed with Christ. If He dwells in me and I am miserable, drowning in the world's problems, exhausted, and without rest, I do not fully believe.

I know, number four is hard. Because once again, I am saying, "It's not them. . .it's you." And I am not blaming us for trespasses against us, illness, or brokenness; but what if I am? What if the truth is, when we said yes to Jesus and invited Him into our hearts, we simultaneously said, "Now I can walk on water!"

And all the readers say, "This woman's cheese has slid off her cracker. She's lost her mind." Yes. I have. I have lost my mind, and now it is fully consumed with the mind of Christ. And He did some whack-a-do things. So, this time you can blame Jesus. But don't blame Him when you sink. He told us how it could be, but we decided how we should be, and our lives are the fruit of that decision.

We, the Christian species, chase rest. We are killing ourselves to arrive at the promises of Christ. Even after discovering Grace and knowing I could not pay back the cross so I might as well calm down, I met with the same issues I always had. I was still afraid.

If you have a nightmare that wakes you from a deep, dreamy sleep, you're exhausted the next day. If you say you believe in the promises of Christ, but your subconscious mind is constantly arguing with your conscious mind about harsh realities, you are never fully at rest.

What do hippies have that Christians do not?

Love.

Christ is the way, the truth, and the life (John 14:6). I am not here to talk you out of that but to further convince you of that. He meant what He said and He said what He meant. I'm not saying you don't love. What I am saying is that it is time to implement love into every aspect of your life until your RAS is continually nagging the subconscious to spy love in everything. When we are finished, there will be no more struggle or doubt, and you will either be water walking or choosing to stay in the boat. The truth will not let you rest until it has completely enveloped you. I do not say this because of my ability to write fancy. I say this because Jesus promised it, no buts (2 Peter 1:4).

Luke had rest because that was the reality of his life at the ashram. There was no nightly news, no social media, and no stress. His life at the ashram was lived in a valley in the beautiful mountains of Colorado. No matter which way one turned on the campus, the glory of God's creation was everywhere. Luke did work: he tended the garden; cooked gorgeous, healthy meals; and taught yoga and philosophy. But the world outside was not a burden to him. He was not consumed with mortgages, delinquent children, car payments, negative news reports, a crotchety boss or spouse, hurried schedules, or questions about what he believed. He was living and experiencing a life of rest, and in turn rest was the foundation of his existence. Peace, man.

I, on the other hand, was writing freedom words and researching Jesus and rest and was run down and worn out by the world. Luke's rest was real; I am not saying that it wasn't. But I am sold on Jesus, and I don't like to be cold. Moving to an ashram in Boulder was not the answer I was looking for. Loving Jesus from the depths of my understanding in steamy South Texas was the only answer for me.

Okay, I know. Yes, this is what the suggestion is, but is there a process?

But of course.

It starts and ends with love.

All the information up to this point has been grounded in scripture with a little bit of science. I am about to rock the boat quite a bit. But I would suggest to you that boat rocking is a good thing. Changing our minds means we must look at things differently. Jesus said this was okay—He told us to do it. But how can we possibly do that when we are telling the mind the same story? If you want different results, you must listen to new information. Annnd. . .the RAS just sent you a warning signal.

"Hey. . .false teacher!"

"Look out! This sounds New Age!"

Chill, RAS. Jesus said we can change our minds (Romans 12:2). I am just going to tell the conscious mind a few things; you can *try* and talk your girl out of them later.

Now if you heard any of the above "warnings," those are indicative of your ability to change your mind despite what Jesus said. If you are running from a new way, it's because your subconscious just yelled, "Fire!"

If you can hear me out, I promise I will back everything I am going to suggest with scripture. In the end, the choice will still be yours. But you needn't be afraid to be challenged; you'll want to love the very idea. Our response is love, no buts.

Initially, as I dug through secular material in search of the difference, my mind was firing objections. I called my good friend and spiritual backboard, who always gets the brunt of my discoveries, edits, and redirects in genius methodology, author and speaker Katie M. Reid. As I unpacked my hypothesis, she listened intently and then said, "Can you back this up with scripture?"

I stopped and pondered. And in a flash it came to me.

"Christ in me, the greatest mystery, the hope of

glory (Colossians 1:27). Believe as if you have received (Mark 11:24). . .and as a man thinketh (Proverbs 23:7)."

And Katie said, "There is your answer."

As a believer, I am responsible for checking my will against the Word. You are responsible for the same. Granted, I am writing a book about it, but you can check my answers. I applaud your efficiency.

My hesitation was that I was diving into unknown waters by looking at my faith through the eyes of science. In my experience, or reality, they were not compatible. How many genius scientists do you know who will argue the existence of a divine Creator over the carbon dating of bones and the Big Bang theory?

The first tidbit that I questioned was a quote by Albert Einstein. Einstein did not profess to believe in a loving, active Creator[3] who was directly involved in our lives. While he did not pretend to worship the God of my heart, he is a lot smarter than I am. Einstein's quote reads, "We cannot solve our problems with the same thinking we used when we created them."

As I battled this, a revelation came to me: that is exactly what Jesus said. "Neither do people pour new wine into old wineskins. If they do, the skins will burst; the wine will run out and the wineskins will be ruined. No, they pour new wine into new wineskins, and both are preserved" (Matthew 9:17).

Still, isn't that what we are doing? Made brand-new when we were saved, yet still battling the world at the expense of rest and bursting at the wineskins? Same

---

3 John Marsh, "Did Einstein Believe in God?" Bethinking, accessed February 14, 2021, https://www.bethinking.org/god/did-einstein-believe-in-god

information, same responses, same exhaustion.

My second revelation came from something else Einstein said, which contradicts the notion that he didn't believe in God: "My God created laws. His universe is not ruled by wishful thinking but by immutable laws."[4] My subconscious instantly read this as God's laws, and then I spilled a glass of water.

I bumped the glass with my elbow, and it fell. The water ran all over the desk and floor, and then the glass fell on the floor. The properties of the water did not change; it was still water, and the glass was still a glass. The liquid contained in the glass took a different form after it spilled, because the force of my elbow moved the glass off its safe setting, and it conformed to the law of gravity.

To negate the laws of earth dwelling. . .good grief, I still can't type *universe* without my brain screaming, "Don't be a hippie!" *To negate the laws of the universe* in the name of my Christian beliefs is no different than saying, "I don't believe in gravity, I believe in Jesus." Yet since God created it, He can defy it too (Acts 1:9–11).

Furthermore, if this is our declaration of faith, none of us should be taking ibuprofen, getting X-rays, using electricity, or boiling water in the microwave. Science, technology, and advancement are part of our existence. I love electricity. You can't convince me to stop using it.

I also love Jesus. I want to progress in that love. So, He leads and I follow. I am continually moved by the

4 "Talk: Religious and philosophical views of Albert Einstein," Wikipedia, last modified July 18, 2020, https://en.wikipedia.org/wiki/Talk:Religious_and_philosophical_views_of_Albert_Einstein

scripture " 'I am allowed to do anything'. . .but not everything is beneficial" (1 Corinthians 10:23 NLT). This is the conclusion I came to as I dove into my research. As I did, another scripture popped into my mind: "See, I am doing a new thing! . . . do you not perceive it?" (Isaiah 43:19).

The standards of the Old Testament Jewish Law are not for us. The laws of the universe, which I fully believe were created by our Creator, are those we must deal with. If you knock a glass off your desk, it is going to fall. We are actively participating in the laws of the universe whether we like it or not. We may as well investigate what that means in terms of our faith.

I want to note this: "Faith is the substance of things hoped for, the evidence of things not seen" (Hebrews 11:1 KJV). Our faith is the hypothesis; it is proven wrong only when we do not advance in the outcome. Stagnation or limbo, want and need, brokenness and turmoil are not part of the promises of Christ. So, are we to accuse Him of lying? Or is there something holding us back from the rest that He pledged His life with?

What is for us is Christ. He is our protector. What is not for us is to abandon His Good Word in exchange for a teaching or life that is all daisies by the world's standards, losing our lives in the process (Mark 8:36). Although to be clear, I sure like painting daisies—but you already knew that.

We can outgrow that which is no longer for us. I will use the pay phone as an example. When I was growing up, my mom always asked me if I had a quarter to call her if I needed anything while I was out. She asked this so often, that it was a rule or law in my life. My mom and I knew if I had a quarter and needed a safe ride or got into a predicament, I would be able to use a pay phone to call home and get help. If you don't know what a pay phone is, you're too young for this book and you're up past your bedtime. March yourself off to bed, missy.

For years after I had my cell phone, I still checked the little pocket in the lining of my purse for a quarter before I left the house. I have never, not once, asked my children if they had a quarter for a payphone. That safe law is of no benefit to them. I ask them if they have their iPhone and charger. But if I said, "Do you have a quarter?" They would say, "I don't know. What can you buy with a quarter?"

Nothing that I am aware of.

I have not spotted a pay phone in years. I don't even know if they are a thing anymore. But prior to the world's ability to be in constant communication with tiny computers in our pockets, the pay phone was the only way to make a call while out and about.

We have outgrown the need to carry a quarter. I also believe we have outgrown unrest. We are going to investigate the new way. It will be better than 5G. It's a direct line to Jesus, abundance, and peace.

A huge part of that peace is to be responsible only for you. All you scripture-memorizing gals came to serve, not to be served (Matthew 20:28). Selflessness is a feather in our Christian caps. But until we are made different, we can hardly serve the world. How can we tell the Good News with joy and authority if we are broken and exhausted? Consider this your spa day. My hope is that when you leave the luxury of the indulgence in self, you will be fully prepared to love well so *the work* will never wear you out again.

That said, I have written entire books on my journey as Luke's mom. It has been a bumpy ride. He is happy, healthy, strikingly handsome, and, as I compose this, most likely swimming with sea turtles in Hawaii, where he now resides. If you are alarmed that his residence is at another Buddhist ashram on the Big Island, don't be. I'm his mother, and I don't worry about my Hippie Baby anymore. How is that, you ask?

All you need is love, man.

This is just getting good.

REST, GIRL REFLECTION

There are four essential parts to the life of rest:

There is no *but* in a good "I love you." Jesus said what He meant and He meant what He said. He loves me. He came to give me rest. No *buts*.

There are only two choices in life: love and fear. Love produces every good thing in life. Fear produces every negative action and reaction.

As a man thinketh, so he is. If I say with my mouth "I believe," but in my heart (or subconscious) I believe my life is falling apart, I am going to fall apart.

Christ in me, the greatest mystery, the hope of glory (Colossians 1:27) means I am consumed with Christ. If He dwells in me, and I am miserable, drowning in the world's problems, exhausted and without rest, I do not fully believe.

DREAM JOURNALING

As you consider the content you have just read, write out any of the words that triggered a reaction in you. Take a few minutes to consider if you are reacting out of fear and if you are ready to move forward in love.

Chapter Ten

THAT'S AMORE!

If I have the gift of prophecy and can fathom all mysteries and all knowledge, and if I have a faith that can move mountains, but do not have love, I am nothing.
1 CORINTHIANS 13:2

There is this thing not visible to the naked eye. You cannot rub your fingers over it, poke it, or squeeze it. This thing has no distinctive smell. It makes no sound. Yet it is not imagined or fabricated. It is an actual thing with tangible power. It can lift us in body and spirit. And it can bring us to our knees. To argue against it or try and stop it would be futile.

This invisible force can be felt from the depths of our creation. It is not animal, vegetable, mineral, or man. We would not exist if it did not. It is the thing that moves my fingers across this keyboard, waking me at 1:00 a.m. to compose another chapter. It provokes, moves, and motivates us. It has an energy we were designed to experience.

It can be recognized but not accurately measured by modern technological advances. It can be monitored by oxygen levels, heart rate, blood pressure, and brain waves. This is not a riddle; everyone knows the answer.

This thing is love.

In the spirit of candidness, I admit that when I wrote those words, I reread them and had the thought, "This sounds like a New Age energy thing." But I bantered back to my RAS and subconscious, *"No, it's not new or old, and energy is a real thing. You can relax. This thing you cannot experience without me, whom I know you are trying to protect, is this thing that I must tell more about. I love you. You are safe and well."*

Yeah, I talk to myself out loud. Just like with the "I am" statements, this has become a necessary practice. The RAS learns from the senses. When it hears me speak, it listens. When I tell it everything is going to be okay and *feel the feelings* of truly being okay, the RAS believes me. It relays the message to the subconscious "Hey, she's good. Look for more reasons for her to stay in this space."

I am changed. More peace and rest come when my mind isn't firing off mindlessly in fight or flight. Fight-or-flight response, which is also known as acute stress response or hyperarousal, is a physiological reaction that happens in response to a threat to survival or perceived attack.[5] This is where I would speak out against basic psychological testimonies. The mind does

5 "Fight-or-flight response," Wikipedia, last modified February 8, 2021, https://en.wikipedia.org/wiki/Fight-or-flight_response

respond to the instinct to brawl or run for the hills, but those are not the only options.

Telling myself "I love you" is a pretty notable change. Do humble, average, everyday Jami Jos say such things? Or is this verbiage saved for rock stars and narcissists? I propose it is for all of us. Granted, the norm for humanity is to browbeat ourselves with our shortcomings, indulge in the testimony of our lack, grapple with self-esteem, and wallow in jealousy and inadequacies.

Yuck.

More unrestful is that we are somehow made greater when we profess our wretchedness. But let me ask you, is it more arrogant to say "I love you. You are great" to myself, or is it more arrogant to say "I am the worst. I am disgusting and pathetic" to the God who calls me His beloved redeemed (1 Corinthians 1:30).

Somewhere along the evolutionary lines of Christianity, we decided it was darling and humble to declare the opposite, in essence to argue with the God of all about who He says we are. We have recited our "humility" enough, clung to it tightly, and it has become our truth. That is how the mind works. It learns from experience. It has only to touch a hot stove or be chased by a dog once to know "Hey, I didn't like that. I am going to look for every opportunity to avoid that mess." So imagine the mind's reaction to being chased by a crazed, rabid dog all day every day and calling it saved? Or worse, calling it wisdom.

An angry mind, one that is a master at condemnation and abusive tactics, is not at rest, because it is not in love with the human it serves. It is simply running on instinct (fear).

Our responses are learned. We buzz along, fancy-free, until someone points out what everyone else is doing, criticizes us, or we just notice that we're different from every other person we encounter. Then the mind takes note. It remembers the way society or our religion says it should be. Its job is to keep you alive and kicking in your environment. You learn not to do fancy and free and instinctively behave the way the world says you *should*.

We adopted Sam when he was nine days old, and I love his gentle spirit. He moves me in a way few humans do. It's not that I love him more than my other children. I just have a tender spot for him and his story. I do not take my role as his mother lightly. His birth mother's decision to place him for adoption was done from the purest of motives, true love. As hard as the story is to tell, I look forward, with cautious trepidation, to the day Sam is old enough to understand how greatly he was loved. I want Sam to know that his birth mom loved him more than he can even fathom. She wanted him to be safe and not to go without. As much as her arms would ache to hold him, she wanted him to be held by someone who could do what she could not.

Sam loves mashed potatoes as much as I love Sam. On a scale of one to ten, it is a tie of one billion to one billion. At dinner, Sam sits next to me, a compromise we reached so that Charlie could look at me while he eats.

I love sitting next to Sam when he eats, but especially when he eats mashed potatoes. With every bite, Sam hums. The little-old-man sounds bubble up from deep within him. It's the sound of bliss. By societal standards, making noises when you eat is not acceptable. But don't you dare tell him this. No one say a word. It's the most innocent, grateful, and indulgent sound I have ever heard. It is not musical or contrived. It is simply a "rude" little instinct that Sam expresses when he meets with a hot bowl of whipped potatoes.

Eventually, maybe right before I die, this social faux pas will need to be corrected. Heaven forbid they serve mashed potatoes at his wedding, and he is hunched over his plate singing to his smushed spuds, inadvertently professing his undying adoration for his first real love. For now, I want him to stay in the innocent mind space of free love.

I use this anecdote to pose a question. Do you love you? When you indulge in that which brings you joy, do you feel compelled to condemn yourself? Let's take that a step further: Do you believe it is arrogant to love you?

This is important because you cannot give to others what you don't possess. And you are love—because you were created by love. God is love, and you are His likeness (Genesis 1:26). Denying that truth is a conflict within yourself. Battling it is a no-win situation, one that creates more unrest. Of the battles I have fought, swimming upstream against the essence of who I am in Christ was the most life-sucking, exhausting feat I have encountered.

And yet, I was used to it. It was my perpetual state of existence. I essentially thrived in the stress of trying not to be who I am and instead to be something I believed the world said I should be. Professing the truth of who Jesus says I am was big work. I would be notably blushed and embarrassed to hear myself say the words "I love you, Jami."

It's ironic. When I was handed my babies, my prayer for them was and still is that they would know and love God, and that they would be true to themselves and their passions and convictions. Yet, from that moment on, I would profess their wonderfulness and remind them to stay humble and small. Jesus did say the last would be first and the first would be last.

I would also note that He didn't specify who would be which.

Loving who I am, focusing on the truth of my creation and life in Christ, doesn't make me a crazed egomaniac. In fact, is this humble to say? I believe I am more approachable, more loving, compassionate, empathetic, sympathetic, and peaceable since I began the practice. And you can be too. Why is this? I propose it is because we are at our best when we are *deciding with God* instead of squabbling with Him.

Let it be said of our unrest that there is nothing as tiresome as barking at the Creator of the moon. Rest begins in our submission to our greatness because of who we are in Him. If that aspect of stress—where negative self-talk is your constant companion—became a space where you were convinced "I am okay," what would your life look like?

In my other books, I call this belly button picking. Digging deep into all that's wrong with us and trying "really hard" to be like Jesus is a daunting task. Grace is the space where we are invited to stop trying and start living. I was undone when I realized how much more rest would follow.

In my continued research of the mind, I came face-to-face with a "law" I had not heard of before. In the beginning, I didn't even want to go down the path. But over and over it came up, so I followed His lead, prayed for His mighty protection, and dove in.

Unlike gravity, it is somewhat less obvious, except in magnets. It is the basic principle of like attracts like, the universal law of attraction. I laugh now, because as I sorted notes for this chapter, I found one where I had scribbled "*hocus pocus?*" next to the definition. But under that, I had written pages of discovery and scripture. It was within these notes I found the folly of the world's attractions versus the peaceable place of Jesus and attraction.

The popular secular belief is that if you focus on what you want, imagine it is yours, pursue your ambitions, and pin pictures all over your house of your desired life, it will be attracted to you or magically manifested. I have watched enough YouTube videos to know, sometimes, this works. That is when my notes turned from investigative to dismissive. I do not condone or believe that if we can dream it, we can be it.

We are not wandering this planet to rub lamps or wish upon stars and get what we want, void of work or ethics. One speaker and his message intrigued me so I googled him. Two years after recording his "If you can dream it, you can be it" video, he was in prison for murdering three people. He was simultaneously serving a term for tax evasion, and he had been married eight times. Was this part of his vision board?

From his prison cell, does he still believe that the universe bows to us and our can-do mind-sets and contrives to please us? I don't know. What I do know is that I was led to learn the difference between trusting the laws of the universe and believing in the God who created them. This God, His ways are perfect (Psalm 18:30).

Love doesn't murder business partners. It doesn't defraud the government. And it has healthy and balanced relationships. That doesn't mean that we don't make mistakes in the name of love. After all, we are human. But in our humanness, we are continually looking for ways to experience greatness. No, that greatness is not necessarily fame and fortune, but it is the greatness we were created for.

The intricacies instilled in us when we were knit together in secret is what attracts us to what we love. My daughter Sophie loves the color orange. When we moved into our current house, before a box was placed in her room for unpacking, she painted one entire wall orange. No color she could have picked would have been more pleasing to her and more offensive to me.

Her room is neatly kept. Her bathroom counters, desk, and nightstand never meet with clutter. Every Sunday night, whether she has been home all week or not, she washes her sheets and comforter. She vacuums and dusts her room, scrubs her bathtub and toilet, and gives two things, no longer in use, to charity. She is methodical in her plans and organized in her undertakings. And she loves pumpkin spice orange. . .even in July.

She is attracted to this color and spies it in sweaters, cars, and decorating collectives. Given the choice, Sophie's choice is orange. I could rage against this. When she was younger, I could have tried to talk her out of it. But, like her incessant need for organized cleanliness, it's a part of who she is. I could no sooner convince Sophie the color was repugnant than I could make her change the color of her eyes.

This is the source of much unrest, raging against that which is not ours to change. Ask me again about Luke's decisions to live and worship at a Buddhist ashram, and my response is the same. Granted, I believe he was created to serve and worship. No, I didn't think this would be part of his story. But I taught him the truth. He is a grown man with a beard. I not only do not get to decide what he believes or what moves him, I am not his Savior. I am just his mom.

Rarely does a day go by that I don't receive a message from a reader about a struggle she is facing with one of her children. They are not petitions for advice; usually, they are prayer requests. More often than not, they are laced with the brokenness of fear. Fear that their child has "rejected his/her faith."

And I cannot say this in every email, but I can say it here. Have they rejected their faith? Or have they rejected yours? The thing about faith is it is not one size fits all. It's a journey of discovery. As with any relationship, there's an initial meeting; but to grow into something of real meaning, it must be tested over time.

We don't get to decide. The good news is you can check this off your to-do list! If what we resist persists and what we love we attract, our best bet is love. Raging and fretting over other people's paths is work we are not asked to do. Do you have to toil and trouble over the sun rising or setting? Do you keep a record of how many breaths you take? No, because that is not your job. As much as my children are a part of me, they are apart from me. I don't get to decide, and I can't save them.

I was recently accused of having no sentimentality. Actually, I am sentimental. Obviously, I can be brought to tears when eating mashed potatoes with my eight-year-old. I think this lack that was perceived in me was not a lack of sentimentality; it was a lack of worry. I am not worried or stressed about my adult babies. I didn't birth or adopt robots. I could spend hours a day in the throes of anxiety over where they are, what they are doing, who they are with, and what they believe. But this is not love; this is fear. When I do think of them, I pray they are safe and well.

And yes, I pray they know and love Jesus. But, and I have said this many times, I cannot make them love who I want them to love. Oh, but isn't this a colossal revelation? Many mothers-in-law have met with this trouble. Trying to talk someone out of or into love is a motive rooted in fear. Fear is not for us.

I understand, believe me, that a life in Christ is the answer. And I understand the consequences. You don't have to remind me. Still, I am not the keeper of the stars. I did my best as a mother. I cut the crusts off, prayed with them and over them, sang silly songs, kissed boo-boos, wiped away tears, and powdered their bums. They grew to be young authors and entrepreneurs, combat engineers, yoga instructors, and geniuses. The other two aspire to be a Lego engineer and a fruit-cutting ninja. Despite my efforts, no matter how much I love them or want Jesus to be their best friend, I do not get to decide who they love.

The other thing I hear, and I have perhaps thought myself, is "They accepted Christ as their Savior when they were in middle school. I guess it wasn't genuine." But this worry was remedied in me with this realization: *Is accepting Christ as Savior an act of power? Or was the sacrificial death and resurrection of Jesus the act of power?* You see, the belief in the "yes" to Jesus is not where our freedom comes from. Jesus is the key. To suggest that they said yes to Him, but it "didn't take" is the belief that the action of saying yes is of greater measure than the God the child invited into his heart.

Saving my children is not my job. I am here for my children, grown and school-aged alike. They can call me if they need me. They know what I believe. But I would rather have them in my life than browbeat them into the illusion of love so that I can say, "They are saved and in love with Jesus." What would they even need with this God if they had me to worship? Because I would expect some accolades if I were responsible for their eternity.

My job is love. Love knows no condition. I know, you might get tired of reading it—plus I have a hunch you may not be resting in it yet, so I'll say it again: There is no *but* in a good "I love you."

I love my children. I love Jesus. I trust Him to love my children more than I trust my ability to make them love Him back.

We have an opportunity to rest more and stress less when we recognize the two choices we discussed earlier, the only choices: love or fear.

Love is easily recognized. It feels right and good. Fear is also easy to spy unless it is disguised as love. Fear can do this because it is crafty. A "love" that does something self-serving, manipulative, or painful is fear masquerading as love.

Recently, I had an argument on the phone with one of my adult babies. I am still shocked by the turn of events. Since they were young, my children and I have had few, if any, altercations. It was ugly and harsh on both ends. The call ended abruptly. In other words, we hung up on each other. I sat in my car entirely hysterical. Once I had regained my composure, I prayed, "Jesus, help me."

I heard it plain as day. "Text 'I love you. I am so sorry.' "

I raged. "I didn't invite the attack, and I know I am not wrong!" Again, "I love you. I am so sorry." I retorted, "I will say 'I love you. I am sorry *that you. . .* ' " Ah, a contingent "I'm sorry." No better than a lousy "I love you." Then I felt the words in my bones. "You have two choices: love or fear."

I didn't want to apologize because I knew I was right. I was afraid of losing that ground. And I love my child. That was the bottom line.

With trembling fingers, I typed I LOVE YOU. I AM SORRY. Within seconds, my phone rang. The fear of being wrong or perceived as such had the power to cause chaos, separation, and pain in an otherwise precious relationship with my child. The power of love changed the entire story.

It's interesting that Christians are willing to admit how small they are, weak, powerless, "humble" sinners, but do not make us apologize or admit we are wrong. How is it we can be both steeped in wisdom, the bright shining stars, and simultaneously the bottom feeders of the planet? Asking for a friend.

While I could go on for chapters about love, I will leave you with this: What will you choose, love or fear? If this is the only question you must ask, are you ready to watch your world morph into an unrecognizable path of earth as it is in heaven?

I love that you said yes!

REST, GIRL REFLECTION

You cannot give to others what you do not possess. And you are love. You were created by God, and He is love, and you are His likeness. What do you choose? Love or fear?

DREAM JOURNALING

Write out ten things, yes ten, that you love about you. Can't name ten? Sit still and listen. What does Jesus love about you? Goodness, don't argue with Him. Just write down what you hear.

Chapter Eleven

BRAVE GIRL

There is no fear in love. But perfect love drives out fear, because fear has to do with punishment. The one who fears is not made perfect in love.
1 JOHN 4:18

There is only room for one God in our hearts. He is all-consuming. When He is justly seated above all else, I am at rest. The issue prior to this revelation was that fear sat on the throne of my beliefs. The scripture focus for this chapter is so powerful, I stared at the words for an absurd amount of time before I knew how to proceed.

"There is no fear in love."

My subconscious retorted, but "the fear of the LORD is the beginning of wisdom" (Proverbs 9:10).

Yeah, what about that?

I sat with this for a while longer. Now I have arrived at my peaceable answer. Acknowledging that God has the power to crush me under His thumb establishes that He can destroy me. But knowing of God's love is to know that He won't destroy me (Jeremiah 29:11). I would be a fool to ignore the mightiness of God. I would be a greater fool to make fear the foundation of my relationship with Him.

Welcome wisdom.

Punishment is retribution for an offense. Yes, there are natural consequences for our actions. Some would call this Karma, but I say it's just the way the ball bounces. But when our choices are narrowed to two, fear or love, there is a precise outcome. It isn't a random bounce of a ball or a haphazard exchange for good gets good, bad gets worse. Love is a choice that promotes us to the safety and rest of a life lived with precision. Choosing love is deciding with God. There is no fear in guessing wrong.

The end.

Ah, but if it were so simple.

Notice, I was able to hear and decipher my subconscious's retort when reading the scripture. My mind had an opinion: "The fear of the LORD is the beginning of wisdom" (Proverbs 9:10). Those words were my deep beliefs, a heart issue, and so that was "my" response. I could have left it at that, and from the safety of what you know to be the whole truth of scripture, your subconscious would have volleyed back with "This gal is spot on!"

What we are here to confront is the space where our deep beliefs are not always compatible with true love. Now if this made you squirmy, you have officially stepped into the mind space of voice sorting. We all have an inner voice, and it has been called many things—an angel on one shoulder, a devil on the other or, my favorite, self-control.

It's not really my favorite; it's the worst. Controlling self is a tiresome act. It is the quintessential last mile of a marathon, the nemesis of rest, and the first-prize trophy in the lifetime case of run-down, worn-out, and miserable. When self-control is the goal, unrest is the prize.

When exchanged for self-love, which is the real love of the God who created you, self-control is rapidly removed from your list of burdens. You are self-control because you are love. Let me explain.

I love wedding cake—without almond extract of course. Why is almond extract a thing? Almonds don't go in cake. Please use real vanilla. But I digress. Like mashed potato humming, it is impolite to have more than one piece. If this is not the case, email me.

At a wedding that I had been the planner and florist for, I had my one indulgent piece. I wanted a second, but frankly I was too busy chasing the photographer, organizing table decor, and wrangling guests. After birdseed was flung and the sweet newlyweds made their departure, I was in the back of the venue with the MOB (wedding planner lingo for mother of the bride). She plopped on the couch with a cake box and two forks and patted the seat next to her.

"Oh, Jami! That was fantastic! So beautiful. Weren't those two lovebirds just the sweetest? Sit with me. Let's eat cake."

My subconscious went nuts. "More cake? Are you

crazy? Look at your step tracker! You have walked ninety-six miles today! Are you going to blow that by eating more cake? You have no self-control." My conscious mind said, "Just sit. You can visit and not have any more cake." I peeled the buckles from my aching ankles, and my feet screamed with relief as my high heels dropped to the floor. As we reminisced over the memorable day, we laughed at the mishaps and cried over the sweetness, and I poked my pink plastic fork into layers of fluffy buttercream and spongy, decadent cake.

Subconscious: No self-control.

Conscious: It's just a bite.

Subconscious: You will have to be wheeled out of here on a platform truck.

Conscious: I am only having one bite.

Subconscious: I think you should have twenty bites.

Conscious: SELF-CONTROL?!?!

Subconscious: How often are we at a wedding? Have some more.

Conscious: Ugh, I am the worst. I have no self-control.

Subconscious: You really are the worst.

The subconscious is a mess until you learn to align it with love. The battle for self-control is like arguing with a three-year-old over which sippy cup they want. They don't know, it doesn't matter, and they will most likely change their mind after the milk has been poured. Self-control stops and turns into deciding with God—once you recognize who is saying what. . .and why.

The conscious mind is the calorie counter of wedding cake consumption. The subconscious is the record keeper or Weight Watchers calculator. The Holy Spirit is the voice of love. When separated, they can be deciphered. When there is no separation, there is just the exhausting, noisy battle over will. In the heat of that battle, the Holy Spirit is silenced. He doesn't bark or howl, "STOP EATING CAKE, YOU HOG!" He just waits for me to get still and know He is there (Psalm 46:10).

In that stillness, I decide with God, and there is no struggle. Wedding cake was not meant to be a moral battle of the wills. It's simply cake. Its power to make or break me only exists when I deem the cake more powerful than the God of my heart. As a man thinketh applies here too. If I believe I have no self-control, I don't.

Much of what I am suggesting goes against that which we have clung to as truth. I know, your head might be spinning. But I would like to suggest you say these words: "I get it. I believe. I choose love. I am love. This is not beyond me."

And it isn't beyond you, but the subconscious doesn't like change. It will rear its ugly head and tell you that you need to stay right where you are. If you have been in hot pursuit of self-control for longer than you can remember, what I am suggesting is rubbing your subconscious the wrong way. Its comfy routine is the pursuit of self-control. It is actually firing in fear because that is what experience has trained it to do.

The subconscious doesn't know what it would look like to just have another piece of cake, because it has never simply had more cake. It has been inundated in what it should do, what is appropriate, and how many calories are involved. The decision to have more of something I love with an old friend I adore and rehash a dreamy evening of new promises and the hope of grandchildren because it is lovely and fun is foreign, even life-threatening, to the subconscious. I might as well say, "I am going swimming in the shark tank to look for rattlesnakes."

But when the noise subsides and the alarm bells stop banging, love is the choice. The clarity only evades us when *Liable Love* comes into play. Liable Love is love for a person, place, or thing that moves God from the highest place in our hearts to second, third, or dead last. Liable Love is a love that is *accused* of "fulfilling" us. The issue with this type of singled-out love is that we deem it more powerful than He who is Love.

When marked, Liable Love doesn't stick around (the cake is all gone) or produces unwanted results (up three pounds), and we no longer are fulfilled. And what do we do? We go looking for more. Exhausted and unfulfilled, we trudge on in hopes of finding more love to hallmark. Friend, you are filled up on, overflowing with, and pressed down in satisfying love.

Rising to defy what you love, whether it be for self-control or self-righteous denial, leaves us in a constant fight to be filled up again and again. From the head of the table, after a big Thanksgiving dinner, we might spy one last piece of cake. But it isn't a battle over "should or shouldn't," it's simply the fullness that keeps us from crossing over and eating something we don't even really want.

When we are in a fight with ourselves over Liable Love, we are grounded in fear. *"I love this thing so much. . ."* What if I never get invited to another wedding? What if the next wedding I go to is one of those Texas Bar-b-que weddings, and they have banana pudding instead of wedding cake? What if I gain weight? What if. . .ugh.

Come back to What If Wow. Because, really, love is the wow factor.

What if you get invited to a wedding next week? What if you go to a Texas Bar-b-que wedding and they have both banana pudding and wedding cake? What if you lose ten pounds because you walked ninety-six miles and had cake? What if you sit with your dear friend and enjoy her company, have some cake, and eat it too?

In a flash, the battle is won. I don't know or care how much cake is satisfying. I love it, and I don't need it, but I enjoy it. Needing love is Liable Love, and it is reserved for the God we are asked to love with all our hearts and all our minds (Matthew 22:37).

The trouble with Liable Love and human relationships is that there is a chance the love will not be reciprocated or it will end. This is a hurtful space. But if you brand someone with the mark of fulfilling you, you have handed them a heavy burden, and you're in for a broken heart. Humans were not meant to fulfill us; they were meant to accompany us. They are part of the human experience, the frosting on the cake, but they are not the plate. If I place a piece of cake in your bare hands, you will get cake all over you. Your hand will be sticky, and crumbs will slip through your fingers. To save the cake, you might hold it tighter or rashly shove it in your mouth. Regardless, it's a mess. But if I put the cake on a plate and hand it to you, the plate will keep the cake neatly for you. It will be the foundation on which the thing you love rests, and you can relax and enjoy it.

Humans, even the most amazing ones, can never fulfill that which only God can fulfill. My friend's teenage son was in an icky relationship with a girl from his school. One night after she had humiliated him in front of his friends, he came home distraught. My friend and her husband asked him, "Why don't you just break up and move on?" And he said, "She's my first love. I don't want it to be over."

First love is a thing, but it needn't be a Liable Love.

Fully aware they could not make him stop loving her, but in the hopes of helping him decide, they asked, "What don't you want to be over?"

"I like having a girlfriend."

"So, you don't want to be alone?"

"Yes, and she is really pretty."

"What if she wasn't really pretty? If she lost her good looks, what else do you enjoy about her?"

He had no answer. The truth was, she was not nice to him. She had a cruel sense of humor, and she lacked maturity and compassion. The greater reality was that he'd burdened a fifteen-year-old girl with the task of fulfilling him with only her pretty face and lousy company to aid her. This left him empty, and he was created to be filled up and overflowing.

Created by Love to love. When we misinterpret love or make the object of love a case for love, we will be left wanting more and accusing ourselves of having no self-control and never being satisfied. This is not rest.

Ending some liable relationships is often more

complicated than shooting a late-night text to break up. Sometimes the relationship can be changed simply in how you perceive it; other times, it takes a court order. But again, the choice is between fear and love. Fear asks what life will look like when you are no longer involved with a particular person. And fear nags for a replacement for the void. Love knows that all things work together for good (Romans 8:28). Love decides with God that while this is permissible, it is not of benefit to me.

By the same token, we can have a Sacred Scar. A Sacred Scar is something that happened to us in the past, and we have given it preferential treatment in the scope of our memories. It's our thing. While trauma to the body can and does happen, it is not the hallmark of who we are.

A Sacred Scar is often encouraged and given further authority in talk therapy. During my graduate studies, this was a technique that never really sat well with me. It is the counseling practice of continually revisiting trauma to overcome the trauma. I am not suggesting that you never bring up past hurts. And I am not saying that talking through an event and the feelings associated with that event doesn't help. But there is a fine line between remembering and marking an event as the thing you cannot ever get over.

If you don't like the way that sounds, you may be carrying a Sacred Scar with you in your back pocket. At a dinner meeting with a colleague and her new husband, we chatted over appetizers, and I inquired how she and her husband met. The gist of the story was that she had been previously married with three children for seventeen years when her husband left her for another woman. After he left, he filed for custody of the children, leaving her neck-deep in legal bills and credit card debt, unable to pay the mortgage. The story took up the rest of dinner. Finally, as we were leaving the restaurant, I said, "You never said how you and your new husband met." She chirped, "Oh, we met at a divorce recovery group at my church. We got married on a private island and honeymooned on his yacht!"

That was the part of the story I really wanted to hear! A couple of months later, I met her again, this time alone for coffee. I leaned in to hear great tales of a romantic cruise on a luxurious yacht, champagne, caviar, island-hopping in the Caribbean, and my favorite, a restoration story.

This was not on the menu.

No, she spent our entire time together repeating the entire story of her divorce and her ex's betrayals. She cried into her mocha latte about the brokenness she harbored, the hate she held for her ex-husband and his mistress, and the long journey she was on to learn to trust. The dialogue was laced with "my counselor says," followed by "never recover," and "can't get over. . ."

I hugged her as we parted ways, determined at our next meeting, I would get the goods on this beachside wedding and honeymoon.

I never did. We met no less than ten times over the next three months. She never asked about my work, family, or children. She never catered to my need to hear about her wedding, extravagant honeymoon, or newfound love. Had she not introduced me to her new husband at that first dinner, I would not even know his name. Her ex-husband's name, Clint, that I knew. I knew where he worked, I saw pictures of Clint and his girlfriend, I read their Facebook posts—Clint and "the tart" were vacationing in Florida and house hunting in Sugarland. I knew he snored and needed knee surgery again.

But we never got past the Sacred Scar to hear the story of a new beginning. She moved to Sweden, got divorced, and I have never heard from her again. Darn it if I would not have loved to hear about that white beach wedding. Greater, I wish she could have lived happily ever after with her dashing, independently wealthy new husband. I forget his name. I don't know for sure, but I can't help but wonder if what's-his-name got tired of his love being neglected for the Sacred Scar of Liable Love lost.

There is room to talk about past hurts, but the story of our restoration is the happy ending we all long to hear. The greatest story ever told wraps up with a Savior being raised from the dead. That is the best part. The parts where Jesus was battered and bruised are part of the story, but the standing ovation comes when the stone was rolled away and the characters report, "He is not here" (Mark 16).

Life lived in love might recount the brokenness, but it does not treasure it.

My cousin, a trauma counselor, explained it to me

along these lines: "I ask my clients to give me the headline of their trauma. For example, 'I was sexually assaulted by a coworker.' From that space we work forward on changing the mind about the trauma. In essence, we acknowledge the hurt, and we talk about the healing."

That healing involves being present in the here and now. Being present allows you to ask, moment to moment, "Am I choosing love or fear?" If we are racked with anxiety and worry that the trauma is going to happen again, we spring into perpetual fight-or-flight coping mechanisms, and we circle the mountain of worst-case scenarios.

However, if we are choosing love in any given moment, we are blazing down the highway of healing. And love heals. In this calm, restful place, when the subconscious screams, "Danger!" we can decipher if we are really in danger and need to skedaddle or if we are safe in the arms of love, here and now, where the past cannot harm us.

I heard a speaker once ask, "If you have a dream where you are being chased by one tiger and the next night you have the same dream where you are being chased by ten tigers, in which scenario are you in the most danger?" I, of course, thought the second! Ten tigers are much more dangerous! But the answer is neither. Dream tigers aren't a real threat. And your Sacred Scar only has power when you believe it can eat you alive.

It can't. It won't.

You are armed with the power of Christ.

REST, GIRL REFLECTION

There is no fear in love. There is no room for Liable Love or Sacred Scars in the perfect embrace of this perfect God.

Rest there, love.

DREAM JOURNALING

Do you have a Liable Love that you feel fills you up? Do you have a Sacred Scar that you have given power to? Write out a prayer to the Father who restores and ask Him to help you decipher the roles these characters or events play out in your brain space.

Chapter Twelve

AW, THANKS

Rejoice always.
1 THESSALONIANS 5:16

Our brains are magnificent. Wow, I never thought, with my many learning struggles, that I would ever say such a thing. But as I have delved into this study, it has become so obvious to me what a wonder the brain is.

I can write and speak this information to you and never have to remind myself to breathe or blink. At the same time, my young sons are playing in the next room. I can be completely lost in creation, but if one of them screams or suddenly it becomes suspiciously quiet, I will be alerted to that. . .*quickly*.

I nearly didn't use the quote from Einstein earlier in this book because I wanted it to be saturated in scriptures and the teachings of Jesus. But when I stopped and really processed it, I realized that was a habitual belief. As I mentioned in chapter nine, Albert Einstein did not believe in a personal God, so in the past I would have, almost robotically, written off anything he said as unimportant to my beliefs.[6]

But what Einstein lacked in belief, I lacked in understanding. I can't expect every person on the planet never to explore the world around them on their own. Face it, every relationship is built on discovery. This is how we come to know someone better.

During this journey, my eyes have been opened to discover new things about God. Some of that just ended up being from a secular view. I'm not adding a beaker of some foreign chemical to the Gospel. What I am doing is exploring more of this God and all He created, without putting my limiting beliefs on Him. Which brings me to lemons.

If you had never tasted, seen, smelled, or held a lemon and I were to try and describe every aspect of a lemon, you might have a general idea of what it was. I could show you a picture, and you might say, "Oh, okay. So that is a lemon."

If you have no experience with lemons, no feelings associated with lemons, it is just a picture of a yellow piece of fruit. But, if you have ever licked a lemon, you will probably have a *physical* reaction to the picture. You might automatically get a twinge in your jaw from the sour juices, or your mouth might begin to water at the thought. You have feelings about lemons that trigger the mind to set off a physical reaction in

6 "Religious and philosophical views of Albert Einstein," Wikipedia, last modified January 8, 2021, https://en.wikipedia.org/wiki/Religious_and_philosophical_views_of_Albert_Einstein

preparationfor a sour taste explosion. Your mind knows about lemons.

Furthermore, if you are full or have recently eaten, the mind might tell the body not to respond, which is just as incredible. The mind knows the body is not in need of anything right now and says, "Don't eat that. . . you are full."

Goodness, the mind is powerful.

If you have ever sucked on a lemon, I would be hard-pressed to stop you from having a physical reaction to a picture of a lemon. Similarly, if you have negative associations with a past event, such as a law-bound teaching about Jesus, whether you were aware of them or not, it can be difficult to change your mind about the feeling without enlisting some new feelings.

So, if all you ever tasted was a raw lemon, and I told you about lemonade or lemon cheesecake, without having experienced them, you might have no interest in taking a big mouthful of those concoctions. But if you decided that your mind could be changed, and you decided to go deeper and "taste and see," you would discover that while lemons are strictly sour, if you add new ingredients, you get to reap the benefits of lemons and have a sweet and refreshing drink or a delicious, creamy dessert!

Yeah, this is a book about rest, not cake and pie.

However, if your unrest is associated with sour beliefs, and that old mind created some of the problems you are now facing, a new way of thinking is the key to solving them. That thinking starts and ends with gratitude.

When we say thank you, in our mother tongue, the RAS and subconscious are seasoned in the flavors of thanks. Together, they know this means you are responding to a need or want fulfilled. When the RAS and subconscious hear you constantly complaining, rehashing grievances, and recounting lack, it believes you are not safe, well, and protected.

By giving thanks in every circumstance, the mind is led to believe you are happy, healthy, and well. While the mind is stubborn, we have established that it can be retrained. It is easily tricked into certain things. Gratitude is the master technique. This brings me to my most favorite and life-changing aspect in my pursuit of rest. What would you say if I told you that the greatest prayer of your heart had already been answered? You don't ever have to worry or think about it again. It is finished.

I propose you would thank me. Don't. I didn't really do anything.

But Someone did. Jesus tells us in Mark 11:24 (emphasis added): "Therefore I tell you, whatever you ask for in prayer, *believe that you have received it,* and it will be yours." Make note of this: rest is belief that there is nothing to fret over. Who better to fulfill the promise of a worry-free, restful existence than Jesus? Gratitude is an essential part of how we are going to step into the crystal-cool freedom of rest. Gratitude is the celebration and praise that allow every other thing to flow in us and through us.

On top of dyslexia, I have what falls under the category of ADHD. I am a one-woman circus. I run on about five hours of sleep. I don't recommend this. I get tired. My brain hardly ever shuts off. If I am not thinking of my next big writing project, I am elbow-deep in paint, working on my next big art project. If I am not doing either of those, I am thinking about how I am not doing those two things and wondering what to do next.

When I started to practice what I am now preaching to you, this was my greatest hurdle: trying to wrestle my brain into submission. I would light a candle. Then I would put some lavender essential oil on my temples. I would get comfortable and try to be still and not think. But then I would think about whether I was thinking. And if I did stop thinking for more than two seconds, I would think, "I am not thinking!" Then I would think about how I almost stopped thinking until I started thinking about not thinking. *Exhausting!*

However, I was able to jump this hurdle with a three-step process I call the Gratitude Shift. *Shift* is an acronym that alerted my brain to a new way of thinking when it came to rest and thanksgiving:

gratitude SHIFT

- Still and...
- Hush your mind with an...
- Intentional override by...
- Feeling
- Thankful

Still and Hush: I stopped worrying about thinking. I just stayed still while thinking. I stilled my body and hushed my busy mind with calm words not cruel words. Instead of scolding my mind, "Jami, shut that brain up, will you?" I spoke kindly, like my heavenly Father would want me to. "Jami, God has given you a brain that won't quit; that is a gift. But you can rest that mind of yours in the endless comfort of thanksgiving instead of letting the vicious cycle of worry rob you of rest."

This first step of the Gratitude Shift—Still and Hush—doesn't mean you roll over and play dead. Quite the opposite. Step one is literally thinking, "I am just going to sit still," without bullying your brain. Trying not to think is like trying not to breathe. The brain has stuff to do. Let it do it. There is no right or wrong way to get still. Just sit. Choose to shift into a lower gear so you can unlock the untapped potential of gratitude that is already all around you. Which leads us to our next step.

Intentional override: From my still and semi-hushed state, I did an intentional override by giving thanks. Instead of focusing on lack and worrisome situations, I took inventory of the abundance that was already present through God's limitless love.

Step two is to intentionally list things out loud that you are thankful for. Now this is my example; your gratitude list will look very different. Your cat may be the greatest blessing in your life. Jesus knows you. He knows your heart and your desires. You are just going to cut loose and give thanks. On my list, I began with Justin, and before I knew it, I was in a celebration "trance" of gratitude. When I ran out of things to give thanks for, I sat still and waited.

Sometimes nothing would happen. Well, except I experienced peace and joy and more gratitude. Other times a scripture would pop in my head, and other times, an idea. This gratitude space is a blast. I look forward to this time, and I do it on purpose twice a day, once in the morning and once before bed. Now it has become such a habit, I do it almost constantly. I practice gratitude if I am upset or restless, and the great thing is, it's free. So even if you are broke, this is available to you. And this is paramount—if you are plagued by unrest, that is even more reason to give thanks for what you do have.

Now for the last step of the Gratitude Shift. It's important because we've been taught to give thanks and count our blessings, but what comes next goes one step further, and it's such a delightful part of the process.

Feeling Thanksgiving: FEEL all the FEELINGS of your thanksgiving.

When I first began the Gratitude Shift, we were in a horrific financial situation. I sat down to have some quiet time alone with God (step one: **S**till and **H**ush), and I began to give thanks through my awareness of the abundance around me (step two: **I**ntentional override). Then I invited my whole self to feel the feelings of gratefulness (step three: **F**eeling **T**hanksgiving).

Like I said, I started with Justin. . .

Thank You for Justin. (He makes me feel so loved.)

Thank you for. . .and I listed each of my children and

their spouses. (They are so fun and talented. I feel so happy they are my people.)

Thank you we have everything we need at this moment. (I feel safe and loved.)

Thank you for my car.

My car. . .

And that's when I thought, *Wait a minute. I own my car.* We have Justin's truck and Sophie's car. My parents have two cars and live less than a mile away. . . . I don't even like that car. I am going to sell my car! Now this was several months ago, and like I said, we were in a huge mess. But it wasn't until I got still and started giving thanks that divine inspiration led me to the conclusion that I could sell my car!

Long story short, this got us out of a jam. It bought us several weeks of freedom from worry. Then, out of nothing, with no sensical reason or way out, we had enough funds to get completely out of the jam and get me a new car. The car I had wanted for a very long time.

In the interim, I gave thanks for the extra money that was available through the sale of my car. Every time I needed to go somewhere or needed something, I gave thanks for how transportation was made available. Every morning I gave thanks that eventually, even though I didn't know how, God would provide. He had a plan.

I would say, "Thank You for provision! You always provide!"

This could be a nod to how easily I am swayed or the power of gratitude, but after a couple of weeks, I told Justin I was going to run to the store. I got my purse and walked outside, and I kid you not, I was baffled that my new car was not in the driveway. I went back inside and got Justin's keys. And he said, "Did you forget we sold your car? It has been a couple of weeks?" And I said, "No, I thought I already got my new one!"

I was overjoyed by the fact that I had convinced my subconscious; I was so submerged in gratitude, there was no lack. I laughed all the way to the store. My heart was bursting with thanksgiving. I was walking on water, and I had so fully stepped into the reality of belief, I did not sink. Instead of recounting the lack, I was celebrating abundance.

If you are a parent or if you can even pick a great love in your life, what would or wouldn't you do for that person? Now, answer me this, why do you doubt that God will do anything you ask of Him?

He said He would. He can do anything. He told you that you could move a mountain into the sea for goodness' sake! All you have to do is believe. Lack is simply the sour fruit of unbelief. Unbelief keeps us in lack and binds our hands and feet, the hands and feet that Jesus wants to use to love others through us. OR it is the deep belief you aren't supposed to have what you truly want or need. And this, my friend, is the opposite of rest.

I want to interject that, when He doesn't answer the way we had hoped, it doesn't necessarily equate a lack of faith. God's ways are perfect. He is good. He has plans and a future for you. If you are ill or lonely, shifting from worry to gratitude is an act of faith and trust.

I believe you were meant to do His work. You are chosen, called out, set apart to spread the Good News.

If you are waiting for your ship to come in so that you can finally get to whatever it is that you want to get to or you are sick and suffering, waiting to be healed, you are invited to give thanks and feel the feelings as if those things have already transpired.

It makes no sense that Peter could walk on water. It goes against every reasonable law. But Peter did walk on water. It wasn't until he relied on his past experience and applied logic and opinion—more than he allowed himself to experience the miraculous—and felt the feelings associated with those ingrained beliefs that he sank.

I told you we were going to change our minds. So, change your mind about gratitude. Test the waters: What greater message can you send the subconscious than to hear the words *thank you* for something it cannot taste or touch as if you have received it?

For example, when I told one of my dear friends about the Gratitude Shift, she started changing the way she journaled. Her brain is busy like mine, so she finds that writing out her prayers and thoughts helps her focus when her brain tries to entice her to focus on unrest instead.

Prior to the Shift, my friend used to write out prayers like this:

God, please provide what we need for a new roof.

God, please give me the creative insight I need to help my coworker with her project.

God, please heal my body from sickness.

Now you might be thinking, What is wrong with

that? Looks good to me. She is going to God with her worries and asking Him for help. I'd propose you're not wrong; however, look at how her prayers shifted when she prayed in love instead of fear and led from a place of gratitude instead of worry:

God, thank You that You are such a good provider and take good care of us.

God, thank You that You never run out of creativity and will supply what's needed for this project with my coworker.

God, You love to heal people. I rejoice that You made me and formed me in Your image and that You know exactly what is going on in my body. Thank You for life and that You are able to restore me.

The Gratitude Shift is not an exercise in controlling God—as if we even could. It's about reminding our whole selves (our minds, our hearts, our bodies, our feelings) what is already true about Him. My friend wasn't trying to play God's hand, but she reminded herself that she was made by and remained in His hand. She went from asking to thanking, from begging to believing, from focusing on what was missing to enjoying what was already available.

When we move beyond *speaking* our gratitude to *feeling* our gratitude, it affects our actions and behavior, and then we start *living* our gratitude. Let me supply you with a delicious example:

My daughter and her husband recently had a hard week and wanted to go out for chips and salsa. They decided to go. They decided to trust that their previous gifts, gratitude attitude, and belief in a generous God would provide means for their tight month. The newlyweds clipped a coupon, added some quarters to their wallets, and went to their favorite Mexican restaurant.

Maggie recounted the experience to me. "We decided to act as if we had enough. We said to each other if we had extra money to go out to eat, we would. We laughed and talked. Then we decided to share a plate of enchiladas. We felt all the feelings of believing we had enough. We didn't stress eat or talk about bills. We took turns listing things we were thankful for and how fun it was to live a life of belief. The feelings took over."

It was then that someone walked past their table, stopped, and said her husband's name. "Christian?" My son-in-law didn't recognize the man at first, but it turned out to be a childhood friend who was now the manager of the restaurant—who comped their meal.

Christian and Maggie laughed, rested, and ate for free. On their way home, they dropped their dinner money in a donation box, because there is nothing more fun than giving from a place of utter cosmic gratitude.

Now I am going to get a little "out there" with you. The bulk of this study is about belief and the need to change our beliefs so that we can experience rest. There are aspects of reality we all must deal with. But I am also going to invite you to pretend. I am not calling you to be irresponsible; you need to live within your means and ask God to guide you in wisdom. But pretend that you have already received in an effort to trick your subconscious into a deeper form of belief.

More than just thanking God for already answering you, I want you to lean in to imagine what it would *feel like* to have received the answer you desire. We get stuck in restless thoughts of unbelief because we cannot grasp how it could ever happen. Remember, the subconscious mind wants to be comfortable. It wants to understand the hows and whys.

Jesus was a storyteller. He explained concepts with parables and knew the value of imagining or envisioning a scenario. I want you to be like Jesus. Tell a story. Experience the prayers of your mouth through the story of your heart. Feel the gratitude you would have if the lump in your throat were replaced with a heart bursting with peace. Move the mountain and walk on the water through the deep belief in your heart.

Truly, what harm does this do?

If we are to have the mind of a child, what does a child do better than pretend? I strongly believe this is a freedom exercise. Have you ever had a song stuck in your head? The consensus is usually to listen to the entire song so that you can move on with your day. So, with a childlike mind, I want you to let yourself and your mind play a little, to "get it out of your system." The truth is when we are in want and lack, we are in a state of idol worship. If we feel guilty or condemned, we are not experiencing the peace Christ offers us.

This is the *key* to believing you have already received—*feeling* gratitude and expectation, but not practicing desperation, frustration, or putting God in a box as to how He will answer. Ask, believing you have received—it's what Jesus told us to do. The pattern I fell into was to ask, then worry, afraid He wouldn't answer. Then I'd call my friends to gripe about the lack. Nothing I have suggested to you is outside the biblical principles you may have memorized. The hardest challenge in all of this is changing your mind without a master plan.

Consider for a minute the placebo effect. The placebo effect is the methodology by which someone is given a "fake drug." For instance, in a study group there might be ten people. Five of them are given a real drug to test its effects. The other five are given a sugar pill. During the study, the participants are measured by the same standards. Many if not all the sugar pill patients experience the same benefits as the real drug participants. Why? Because their subconscious assumes or *feels* the patient is getting the healing benefits of the drug. And they respond accordingly.

The power of the mind is outstanding. The power of feelings cannot be ignored. The power of faith is astronomical. The subconscious mind deals in habits and patterns. You are going to need to give it a sugar pill. I propose that the sugar pill is gratitude. The miracles will follow. Absolutely anything is possible with God. Now, we all say that, but our deep belief is our sinking Peter.

We can only stay on the water instead of under it when we go to the place of unshakable belief. The minute we let the subconscious meddle with the miracle, we are sinking. So, if we gripe and complain, feeling stress and unrest, and then pray with our mouths, "Jesus help," but our deep belief says, "It will never work, my life is the worst, and frankly I'm pretty comfortable here," we are not praying the prayers of believers.

Thank God we are not like that anymore!

REST, GIRL REFLECTION

Give thanks! Feel the feelings of gratitude. Change your mind, change everything!

DREAM JOURNAL

Write a thank-you letter giving thanks for that which you have not yet received. Express every aspect of what it would *feel* like to hand that letter to God. Use present tense words, and experience the joy and enlightenment of its having been answered.

Chapter Thirteen

FOR THAT TOO

Bear with each other and forgive one another if any of you has a grievance against someone. Forgive as the Lord forgave you.
COLOSSIANS 3:13

Let it be said: unforgiveness is a rowdy beast. It will wake you from sleep and devour you in your dreams. Some trespasses are harder to let go of than others. I will be the first to admit my folly in the realm of judgment and unforgiveness.

I was shocked to learn that the average adult makes thirty-five thousand decisions in a day. The shock wore off quickly. Truly, when I thought about it, that number seemed a little low. Prior to writing this chapter, I made four thousand decisions. Shower and get ready? Which chair to sit in, lighting, pee now or later? Coffee, water, or iced tea? But truly, these aren't major decisions. I give them little thought. Also, I forgo peeing nine-thousand eight hundred times a day, because everyone's needs usually trump mine, and I don't have time for basic bodily functions.

So, I just decided not to complain about an ongoing urinary tract infection to talk to you, somewhat seriously, about decision making. There are big ones and small ones. We are currently in the market for a new home, and my beloved husband was still wrapping things up for our West Texas ranch sale when I found our current home. Silly me, I thought that the layout was perfect and the lot was huge. Granted, it's in a golf course community, with a large lot, something my wide-opened-space-loving hubby had never encountered.

But back then, we were starting a new life in the North Houston area, so I was delighted to take Justin on the walk-through of our new home minutes before closing on the property. He was less than thrilled. Justin doesn't understand neighbors. He is a kind human being, but he doesn't chitchat over fences with the guy next door, and I am unable to explain golf-cart cruising to him.

The decision to find my man some acreage is not the hard part. The decision on what will work for our family, finances, and long-term plans is a bit heftier. But as we've discussed in previous chapters, the ease of deciding with God makes the process pretty basic—love or fear. If we are afraid a property is too much to take on, we break down those thoughts into more questions about love and fear. Is it too much for our budget? And we break that thought down further. Do we love having the means to travel and see our children? What sacrifices would we need to make to continue seeing our children? We still haven't found a new home.

But I'm not worried about it. Of course, I'm not at home now. I am in a hotel on the beach writing a book. Justin is back at home with two little boys in a neighborhood that he would be glad to move out of, so he might be a little worked up at the moment. But I texted him to check in and ask what he was doing. Packing. Believing he has received the home we have prayed for, oblivious to the fact that two neighbors have texted me inquiring why Justin is in the garage packing boxes.

Let's just keep that between us. I think it would push Justin right over the edge.

Clearly, the mind shift sometimes must stay in the festivities of hope lest you go completely postal because the neighbors keep having the audacity to say, "Good morning!"

You can pretend, and you can have the mind of a child, but the escape to rest has a menacing deterrent. Unforgiveness.

It was on a trip to Costco—a decision I hate to make, but I love my family, and they love copious amount of Cheez-Its. I prayed a quick prayer. "Jesus, open my eyes to decision making. What does it mean to decide as You would decide? How can I be more in tune with Your decisions?"

Honestly, Costco is not the best place to commune with the Lord. I have zero tolerance for greed. While this might offend a few folks, I have decided to tell you, I have no patience for free samples in public shopping arenas. The licking of fingers, the shoving of children, and the stalled-out lines in front of the aisle I am trying to get to send me reeling. My insides scream, "SERIOUSLY! IS THAT ZAP-FRIED TAQUITO THE END ALL FOR YOU, FOOL?!" Don't worry, I will expose my folly shortly. So, on this trip to the mega trough, I was decidedly cognizant of everyone around me. The first decision I made was to get drinks. As I unloaded an apocalyptic-case of sodas into my cart, I observed a man bark at his pregnant female companion to grab a case of Dr Pepper.

She obliged.

A few aisles down, he stacked a bag of beef jerky onto the heavy cargo she was wrestling.

Then he stopped to graze on a sample of chili, never offering her help or a taste.

Next, I saw him stop to read a bag of chips. Well! Would you look at that, the ape can read. His companion looked weary. He never seemed to acknowledge her but stacked the bag on top of her heavily weighted arms. She adjusted and lowered her chin to secure the items of the cleverly balanced haul.

I bit back fury, and in my mind, I heard, "*And for that too.*"

What?

In the next aisle, a woman was sitting on the floor, eating a tiny cup of some free sample, talking on her phone. Her toddler was beating the dog out of an enormous bag of Doritos. The child and I made eye contact, and I smiled. The little menace stuck her tongue out at me and then said, "You're ugly!"

Hmmm.

"And for that too."

I pushed my cart to check out, where I was met with

the hostile glare of a fatigued, underpaid cashier. Her only words to me were "Card!"

Nice.

"And for that too."

As luck would have it, I exited the store behind the ape and his woman-made-pack-mule. He barked at her, "What the hell did you do with the keys?"

She mumbled, "I think they are in your pocket." He pulled them out and got in the truck and started it. She arranged the items in the back of their truck, stretched her neck, and shook out her exhausted arms. I wanted to help her kill him and bury the body. . .but I had ice cream, and it was melting.

"And for that too."

I drove home, adrenaline pumping, ice cream melting, fully engulfed in disgust, rage, and the promise to never, ever go back to Costco. Sometimes I have a short fuse with humanity.

"And for that too. . ."

I barked, "WHAT IS THAT? WHAT???"

"And for that too."

Later that evening, with exponential amounts of chicken pot pies and Oreos neatly packed away in the pantry and children nestled in their beds, I sat down to write. "And for that too" was the resounding riddle I had to solve. Seriously, I had no idea what this meant. I opened my Bible, and these words jumped off the page: "For Christ also suffered once for sins, the righteous for the unrighteous, to bring you to God. He was put to death in the body but made alive in the Spirit" (1 Peter 3:18).

"And for that too. . ."

For the lousy husbands/boyfriends/baby-daddies, superstore shovers, lackadaisical parents, mean toddlers, and hateful cashiers, yes, He died for that too. And for the judgmental and snarky author, with introverted tendencies and a husband who makes those tendencies shy in comparison, He died, yes, for that too.

I sat in the quiet and made a decision. My thoughts and perceptions have only two choices: love or fear. Which translate to forgiveness or hate. The grandest choice I can make, every single day, is to know that He died for that too. He died for my bad decisions, bad behaviors, and bad days. Furthermore, He died so that I could be brought to God righteous. I know many of you will read this and decide to lose it because (1) you cannot believe the audacity of the man/ape in Costco, or (2) you thoroughly enjoy free-sample grazing at mega stores.

Neither of these things is the point. The real point is I am no better, and I have decided to believe in my righteousness, bought and paid for once and for all through Jesus. And what's greater, those who irritate, offend, and exasperate me, well, He did it for them too. Although it has only been about eleven months since I took on the decision between love and fear, deciding to stop and remember, "And for that too," is a glimpse at what it meant to die for a fallen world, knowing full well that it could go completely unnoticed.

While I still sin, He is available to help me decide. My award-winning fiascoes and sometimes brutal disgust for humanity have nothing on why Jesus was willing to do this thing. This huge thing, this brutal death, for the world He so loved. It is a decision that changed the way we maneuver among humans and make grand choices.

I cannot pretend to understand what you have met with. I do not know who has hurt, betrayed, or abandoned you. You may not like it, and it may send you reeling, but friend, He died for that person too. I didn't write the declaration on forgiveness. I am just here to gently whisper the words of freedom you have been welcomed to. You have two choices: love or fear.

Unforgiveness is a by-product of fear, especially if the unforgiveness is acquired by a Sacred Scar. Giving up negative thoughts about the person who harmed you is part of the conscious mind's comfy routine. Even if the mere thought of that person makes you physically sick, at least the subconscious knows you are about to puke, and it knows how to handle the situation.

Perhaps it is cliché, but forgiveness is not for them, it is for you. If letting go of your contempt is scary, it might be time to ask yourself why it scares you. For me, holding on to a trespass meant that I got to invent scenarios where that person finally "got what they had coming!" But those are dream tigers. They don't really exist, although they kept me circling the mountain of contempt, where I found myself carsick and angry, without resolution.

It was when I applied the "and for that too" method that I first began to really experience the rest of forgiveness. I would like to interject this tidbit: if you have invented a wrathful god who chases down predators and pays them a just punishment for their sins against you, your subconscious is on high alert. Remember, it believes you. And if the god you are talking about delivers harsh, ugly judgments on others, watch out, he is coming for you next.

Let Jesus be Jesus and let Him be all over you.

Moving forward in rest means letting go of the past not repeating it. Definitely learn from it; but offer it to Jesus, and thank Him for bringing you out on the other side. Granted, with one particular trauma in my life, I had to implement words such as "Thank You for freeing me from that hurt. I am so happy and thankful that I have found the rest of forgiveness." I hadn't, but I believed as if I had received, felt the feelings of a bright and restful future, and now when I consider that hurt, I am free from *fear.* And behave as such.

A Sacred Scar, when embraced and nurtured, fosters more fear and manifests more unrest. Again, I don't make the rules. But within this space there is even more good news. Forgiveness isn't an action you must take; it is a thing you possess. This is paramount for the unrested.

Trying to forgive is hard work. Owning forgiveness is like having a nickel in your pocket. It is yours because everything Christ has you have (John 17:10). When we associate our hurt feelings with the act of forgiving, we are left to sort through our inadequacies. For example, I was deeply hurt by a friend who told a lie about me. She apologized, although our friendship was never the same and ended quickly after.

But I own forgiveness. It belongs to me as it belongs to Christ. When I think about the infraction, a lump rises in my throat. The situation was hurtful and embarrassing. I am disappointed by how things turned out. Sometimes, not often but sometimes, I miss her. Do I offer the forgiveness offered to me? Yes. Did I remove this person from my circle? Yes. That toxic relationship is not for me.

I prayed for her, "Go be made well away from me." Free from the burden of unforgiveness, I am at rest. I know that the story she told was a lie, and I know that Jesus died for that too. I chose love and love forgives. I own forgiveness.

This is the sweet slumber of rest. I hear you. "You have no idea what so-and-so did to me!" You're right. I do not know the treacherous road you have walked. But Jesus knows, and still He died for that too. When it comes to forgiveness, I see myself opening a box that belongs to me—a box filled with light.

The vision of the box being opened and all this light pouring out is one I am convinced is the light of Christ. First John 1:5 (emphasis added) tells us, "This is the message we have heard from him and declare to you: God is light; in him there is *no darkness* at all."

I mentioned my oldest daughter and her husband before. Maggie and Christian only recently moved from a second-story apartment, where they had originally been quite miserable. The woman who lived below them was truly one of the most unhappy people I have ever encountered. I saw her only twice; she really did break my heart. I have never seen someone so unhappy, bitter, and angry. Maggie and Christian are a quiet couple. How quiet? Maggie makes hand embroidery for a living. There is no quieter vocation than hand stitching. Christian is a hotel manager and works long hours. When Christian is home, he loves to watch movies, read, write, and go to the park and walk with Maggie. They don't listen to loud music, and they don't have parties.

But the woman who lived directly below them called the apartment manager and the police on Maggie and Christian on several occasions. If Maggie walked across the apartment from her office to the kitchen, the woman downstairs would bang on the ceiling with a broom. If they cooked dinner, she would do the same or call the police. One night, in the dead of sleep, the broom banging began, and shortly after, the apartment was filled with red-and-blue police lights. The woman was outside screaming to the police that she never got any peace because Maggie and Christian were so loud.

In that instance, my son Luke was visiting them, and he had walked from the office sofa to the bathroom. Maggie would call me sobbing, exhausted from the attacks, afraid to go outside, and discouraged that she had to tiptoe to get a glass of water.

Finally, Maggie and Christian went to speak to the apartment manager. The manager said, "That woman is a mess. Her full-time job is complaining. She is not even allowed in this office anymore. We have told her and the police that you aren't doing anything wrong. You pay rent; you can walk to the bathroom and move freely about your apartment."

Maggie and Christian actively started looking for

a little house with a yard. This was during Christian's furlough from work because of the coronavirus. It didn't make sense to move, but they wanted to be free of their current living conditions. Maggie left a couple of firm but kind notes on the woman's door. "We are trying not to disturb you. It is not easy to live in an apartment. We are doing our very best and would appreciate it if you would not bang on the ceiling."

This woman is what I call a peace vampire. These creatures are everywhere. They are quick to bring others around them down. It's as if their misery is more than enough for everyone around them.

The first thing I want to say is this: it is imperative that you have a protective prayer in place to guard your mind and beliefs. One I love is simply saying, "Thank You, Jesus," over and over and over.

Again, in the conscious part of our brain, we can make choices and know we are not having a frat party in our upstairs apartment, but our subconscious or deep belief needs protection from attack so that it doesn't create barriers to our newfound beliefs or desires.

Maggie used gratitude and love to move from misery to peace by doing just that. When the woman downstairs would bang on the ceiling, Maggie would blanket herself in statements like "I love this little apartment. I love that when I look out the window, I can see trees. I love living here with Christian. I am safe. I am healthy. I am moving to a new house with a yard. I am excited to see how this will happen. I pray the woman downstairs finds peace."

Maggie and Christian live in a college town, and most of the rental houses have been harshly treated by the university students. But recently a Realtor called them, saying she had a house that met all of Maggie's wants and needs. As they packed to leave, the woman downstairs banged on the ceiling. When they came downstairs with a load of boxes, she glared and barked, "Good riddance!"

When Maggie went back to get her deposit from the complex, she saw three small children playing on her old landing. The woman downstairs went from having Maggie embroidering overhead to small children running around.

Which brings me to something very important (again), Proverbs 23:7 (KJV), "As he thinketh in his heart, so is he."

If you believe you are miserable—you are.

If you believe you are desolate—you are.

Believe forgiveness is impossible, and it is.

This is the power of belief. The catalyst to change is in you. Christ in you, the hope of glory! The power to forgive and find rest is yours. If you ask and believe as if you have already received, everything is going to change.

Believe you are blessed, and you are.

Believe you are living in peace and rest, and you are.

Believe you belong to a good and loving Father because you do.

Believe without allowing the subconscious to sabotage you, and you will see change.

Believe that forgiveness is yours, and you are at rest.

REST, GIRL REFLECTION

He died for that too. We can embody unforgiveness and end up like the broom-pounding tenant, stuck in a place of unrest. Or we can take the inheritance offered through our union with Christ, believing we have what He has. We can choose a new mind (1 Corinthians 2:16), truly live as a new creation in Christ (2 Corinthians 5:17), and own forgiveness (Ephesians 4:32).

DREAM JOURNALING

Who are you harboring unforgiveness against? Write their name in your journal followed by "and for that too."

Chapter Fourteen

THE ART OF CHILL

Take my yoke upon you and learn from me, for I am gentle and humble in heart, and you will find rest for your souls.
MATTHEW 11:29

Some outside forces may throw you off your groove as you relearn a life of rest. They come up occasionally for me, less and less as I have progressed. This is the first book I have written that is more a testament of my freedom than an erratic unraveling. I've had to rethink some wording so as not to sound too bossy. At the same time, there have been opportunities to witness the practices and implement them even on my short writer's getaway.

I ran to the convenience store last night for some bottled water and upon returning to the hotel, I realized that the clerk had given me change for ten dollars instead of twenty. That is eleven dollars I cannot recoup. And I chose love. I can toss and turn over the mishap, or I can bask in the abundance of rest. What is mine is His and what is His is mine. Bless that eleven dollars.

I was also alerted to a negative Amazon review of my book *Well, Girl*. I read it. This reader/reviewer, who by the way received an advanced copy and didn't even buy the book, left a one-star manifesto about my terrible writing and wayward faith. And. . .*I am just fine.* I know who I am. I know who He is. And I know He instilled in me the ability to write. God alone understands the odds of me sitting on the balcony of this hotel, watching the waves, writing my fourth book.

The wonders never cease.

I can honestly say, as exciting as it is to be writing this book, I am more delighted that I am in no way hot, bothered, hurt, or upset by the review. My book just wasn't for that woman. We are uniquely and individually created by an amazing God.

Three days post the 2020 presidential election, no decision has been made. I haven't really checked much, but when I have, it is obvious that our country is split. More obvious are the opinions about voter fraud, he said/she said, and "what will become of us?"

I am entirely absolved of the fret.

It isn't that I do not care; I care. I care about our country and our future. But I am not worried or distressed. I am at rest in the arms of the true King. This is not the old Jami reporting to you live from Galveston. And I approve of this message.

The old Jami would have called her friend Katie and ranted about the review. I probably would've had a good cry. But the new Jami, a restful Jami, knows that reviews come and go. Books are loved and hated. The words in my head can be words of love or stories of fear.

I must ask, has there been a chapter where I haven't mentioned what a hard time I had in school? I doubt it. But the other day as I was eating lunch with my sister, I remembered something else about school. I pretended I wasn't there. My sister, Stacey, and I played house well past the "normal" age of pretending. She and I both wanted nothing more than to be mommies. We dressed our dolls for bed, and before school we would dress them for "day care" and set them up on the couch with instructions for our mom to care for our babies while we were at "work."

And while it did my academic career no good, I would daydream and pretend I was at work. I think I was an imaginary secretary of something. In my mind, when a worksheet was placed in front of me, I would pretend it was a legal document I was preparing. This probably says a lot about my failures, but it got me through the day until I could get home and do what I really wanted to do, play with my baby dolls.

At one point I wanted this expensive doll from Sears. Y'all, I was old enough that I was making money babysitting the neighbor kids while still playing house. I put the doll on layaway, and then I prepared my room for her arrival. The doll was an older-looking doll than my other babies, so I pretended I was adopting her. Every time I went to Sears, aka the orphanage, I would stop and play with the doll on the shelf as if I were visiting until I could bring her home forever.

Another time my family and I went to dinner at

Red Lobster. Stacey and I brought our babies, and we pretended we were on a cruise. When our family piled in the car, we stood on the wooden plank entry of the restaurant and imagined we were watching whales. The whale was just my dad's 1980 model Ford LTD. It honked, most irritated, and it was time to go home. The vacation was over. Pretending may be for children, but we are going to have a childlike spirit and play a little house. Have you ever heard the saying "Don't dress for the job you have; dress for the job you want?" We are first going to do it with our speech. We are going to speak life and truth from now on.

Just as God moves in our faith, which counts us righteous, where is there room for words like "I never win" or "I have the worst luck!" As a man thinketh? When I expect the worst, I have experienced that I get the worst.

This is good news, because I fully believe if you expect that God will answer you, He will. However, do not believe you know *how* He will answer. This can be a huge stumbling block. We do not get to boss God around.

While I encourage you to talk to Him and pour out your heart, I also encourage you to use words like "I surrender" and "I trust." I like to think of this in terms of a child waiting for a much-wanted Christmas gift. Imagine the child wants to be a chef. They love to pretend they are in the kitchen, crafting exotic dishes. And so they ask for a set of master chef knives. You, the parent, want to bless and love your child. Were you to get them real knives, they would have to go on a top shelf in the kitchen. They couldn't actually play with the knives. And while you want to answer the request, there is not going to be any real fun in the gift of real, razor-sharp knives.

You explain to the child, "I want to bless you. I understand what you want. Can you trust me?" Christmas rolls around and, much to their surprise, there is a set of chef's knives—of course they are pretend. They are play knives that keep them safe and allow them to play the games they wanted to play. They were not afraid to ask for what they wanted. But you, the parent, knew how to best bless them.

This is like our Father God. This is how He answers when we let Jesus be Jesus. We speak life, gratitude, belief, and trust, and then we let Him do His thing. I believe your faith is growing. Now we are going to climb out of the boat. You are going to believe as if you have received.

My mom told me a story years ago that I have always remembered. There was a single mom of three, and she had no groceries. It was nearly time for dinner, and she said out loud to Jesus, "I am setting the table. We are going to pretend we will have a meal." Then she went about the business of preparing for a feast she did not have. She put a tablecloth on the table, set out forks, knives, and glasses for milk. She went so far as to put out dessert plates. The entire time she repeated the words, "I am so glad we have this beautiful meal! I can't wait to taste this food! Thank You, Lord, for such a lovely dinner!"

She said it over and over. She sat at the table, her kids playing in the next room. She continued to give thanks. And the doorbell rang. So confident that dinner had arrived, she hollered to the kids, "Wash up! It's almost time to eat!"

Lo and behold, there stood her neighbor with a casserole, chocolate cake, and a gallon of milk. The neighbor explained she had made the meal for a new mom at church, but the woman's mother decided to stay a week longer, and they didn't need the food. The neighbor asked if the woman and her children would like it. And they did.

What if that hadn't happened? That is not the issue. What will they eat tomorrow? Again, not the problem. The issue, the big problem, is that we can't move the mountains if we are wondering *how* to move the mountain. It is not our business to be God. It is our job to believe.

Hear me when I say some things are bigger than dinner. If you or a loved one is sick, dying, facing a brutal injustice, or about to lose your home, I know this practice might be hard to swallow. I say this with the breath of compassion, not judgment: you can do all things through Christ who gives you strength (Philippians 4:13).

If you must give thanks because you found a mate to a sock, give thanks. If you must give thanks that your crappy car actually started, give thanks. If you must pretend dinner is ready, bless your imaginary food. Dare I say, fake it until you make it. This is how we are going to retrain our minds to stop waiting for the lion instead of looking to the Lamb.

Look, if you believe that Jesus was born of a virgin, suffered, died, was buried, and rose again, you have already practiced rogue belief. I am not here to talk you out of believing in the miracle of Christ, but come on?! Virgin birth? Dead to live again?! What's that all about? So, I ask you, why can you believe that and not believe that you can change your mind and actions to focus on Jesus, abundance, and His miraculous abilities instead of focusing on lack?

One of my most favorite scriptures ever is Hebrews 11:1 (KJV): "Now faith is the substance of things hoped for, the evidence of things not seen."

I encourage you to give yourself some evidence, and increase your faith through actively participating in believing as if you have received. While this may seem old school, if your words are habitually that of lack, get yourself a rubber band and pop yourself anytime you say something negative. That is not the language of the rested. Speak that which is good, pure, holy. Speak to yourself the way Jesus would speak to you.

He encourages you.

He guides you in wisdom.

He adores you.

If you ask Him for a fish. . .He would never give you a snake (Matthew 7:9–11). He is exactly who He says He is. It is when we speak this truth that we will be changed and will experience rest. Recognition is now in your hands.

I crave truth. Most definitely, I want to recognize it the moment I see it. Yes, sometimes the truth is hard to face. Yet, I want to be in the know. As a mom of many, I have a keen eye for a scam. Kids will try and deceive for a variety of reasons. Perhaps, if you are like me, this is your superpower. Certainly, we are all well trained in the saying "If it looks too good to be true, it probably is." Unfortunately, present company included, many of us have taken the bait hook, line, and sinker. But in a year of hyper-unrest, I am totally chill. It seems too good to be true. Still, I believe.

I recognized a new truth when I first noticed that my five-year-old, Charlie, was using the word *recognize* rather frequently. He does this. Charlie picks up a new word and cannot wait to add it to his dialogue. He is a laugh riot with his raspy voice. He sounds a little like he smokes a pack a day. But he also cannot enunciate *l*'s, *D*'s, *W*'s, or *P*'s; and he tends to use a unique pronoun he and his brother Sam have embraced since the first time they communicated. Instead of the usual *him*, *her*, *he*, they use *herms*. "Herms won't share!" or "Herms went to the movies." You get it.

One Sunday when Justin took Sam and Charlie to the park, they returned with Charlie in hysterics. Young Charles had fallen and hurt his foot. According to him, he would "never walk again." This was most likely an exaggeration. A couple hours later, he ran past me in the hall. I chirped, "Oh, thank goodness! You are not crippled for life! Be sure and tell your father; he's concerned." Charlie stopped in his tracks and said, "Nope! Don't tell herm! Wet's wait and see if herm can weckognise I am walkin' just fine!"

I kept the secret. But *recognize* rang in my ears. I headed to my office and added it to my notes. I don't know why; I just knew it would be important later. A little while later, with other things on his mind, Justin was working at the dining room table when Charlie walked up to him and said, "Daddy! Youm didn't eben weckognise that I can walk!" Justin apologized for the lapse in parenting and celebrated with Charlie over the "miraculous" healing. That's when it hit me, and I recognized a huge truth—one I had missed and one my God was eager for me to embrace. Our Father in heaven doesn't miss a thing. I have said this, and yes, I was raised with this truth. But I don't think I really got it until that moment. If I am honest, it took me a full day of pondering and scripture and stewing before I was ready to say it out loud.

Of the emails I receive, it is quite obvious that many of us feel as though God has forgotten or is not paying attention to us. Often, I hear from readers who say, "I don't feel Him near. . ." or "I feel so far from God right now."

I know; I have been there. But I am certain I will never feel that way again.

Bold?

Yes.

No, that doesn't mean that I won't face my share of trials. But what I didn't recognize until Charlie starting using "weckognize" was that God doesn't move away, I do.

And this is big. Over and over, I have noticed scripture and teachings about our unity to Christ; I just haven't wholly applied it. And by applying it, I mean instead of chasing Him and justifying Him, I haven't rested in His presence.

I ask Him for help, and then I jump straight into my worries and humanness and wait for a thunderbolt.

When the thunderbolt doesn't arrive, I testify to the lack. And I am embarrassed to admit, I can picture Him at the dining room table saying, "Yes, I heard you. I am right here. . .stop, slow down, let's just be."

But I have things to do, places to be, and I dwell in the comfort of my struggles.

Yes, I know that one is still a little hard to swallow. However, I am convinced that the past is more comfortable than the unknowns of the future. Recounting and dissecting the past is a bad habit, one that makes the future seem scary.

I mean, I know what I have failed at—and I'm confident in most cases that I won't make the same mistakes a third or fourth time. I know who to walk away from and who to count among my friends. But I also know I have gotten a little less brave and a little more recluse from the wounds.

Still, it is those things that keep me grounded in the past instead of boldly rushing into the future. If believing God is the catalyst to doing brave things, I should have already ordered my parachute and been ready to brave the heights. Not really, you are not getting me to jump out of a plane, no matter how much I love Jesus.

But I know He wants me to recognize Him in me. He wants me to believe that mountains can be moved. More importantly, He invites me to imagine it as if it were already done—let go of the side of the plane and jump.

While I am not much for resolutions, I have resolved never to question His presence again. This is my bold new recognition. Not only can nothing separate me from His love, nothing can separate me from Him.

He is right here.

Right now, at this moment.

I cannot hide from Him.

And I don't want to.

What I have spoken in the past is a lack of Him—a need to get more of that which I am already drenched in. Granted, this fills pews and collection plates. It's a big-ticket price on the how-tos of getting more of that which was already bought and paid for. Don't get me wrong; we need church, and the Body is important. But I will no longer ignore the power that is so much a part of me that I wouldn't recognize myself without Him.

Obviously, I am a firm believer that we are what we speak. Were I to profess that He is not near, I recognize I am ignoring the Truth of who He is and why He died for me. The veil was torn. The sacrifice was complete. Now He calls me friend. The least I can do is recognize that He is right here.

When I acknowledge Him, rest is mine.

REST, GIRL REFLECTION

Speak that which is good, pure, holy. Speak to yourself the way Jesus would speak to you. And above all, recognize He is always right here.

DREAM JOURNALING

Write out this scripture: "Complete my joy by being of the same mind, having the same love, being in full accord and of one mind" (Philippians 2:2 ESV). Write out what it looks like to speak and think as Jesus would.

Chapter Fifteen

WORRIED GIRL VS. INSPIRED GIRL

"No eye has seen, nor ear heard, nor the heart of man imagined, what God has prepared for those who love him."
1 CORINTHIANS 2:9 ESV

We have established that the subconscious wants to keep you safe, and safe means familiar. The subconscious is like a child. It believes in what it experiences, which is why the concept of Santa Claus is effective with young children. If you tell your child that a fat man in a red suit is going to come down the chimney and deliver toys, and they go to bed and wake up to new toys, they believe in Santa. A child that has heard of Santa but wakes up to no toys finds that harder to believe.

As a child grows and has experiences that prove to him or her that this is not plausible, they are hard-pressed to believe in Santa Clause anymore. While it is very exciting to think that we can live a life of rest, the subconscious of the adult brain is like a child who has just walked in on you putting toys under the tree and eating the cookies. It has seen too much. Perhaps it has known too much hurt, disappointment, or unanswered prayers. But we are going to use the imagination to help you retrain that part of your brain. Once your mind is organized, rest is your constant companion.

Christopher Bergland wrote the article "The Neuroscience of Imagination" in 2012 for *Psychology Today*.[7] He wrote, "Creativity is the ability to bring together disparate [or contrasting] ideas in new and useful combinations."

When you use the imagination to play out scenarios, the subconscious does not decipher between reality and imagination. This is why your body responds chemically, increasing the heart rate, nausea, and sweating, in response to a bad dream or imagining a fight with your mother-in-law. Or why your mouth waters if I suggest you bite into a lemon. You didn't bite into a lemon, but you still had a physical reaction.

This is good news because it means if you feed the subconscious good visuals and verbal cues, it is going to believe you. Furthermore, the subconscious wants you to feel good. Currently, the subconscious believes that you thrive in worry. Prior to understanding this information, the subconscious believed that worry was your "go-go" juice. You are going to continue to tell it a new story.

Using the What If Wow method is the active practice

---

7 Christopher Bergland, "The Neuroscience of Imagination," Psychology Today, February 8, 2012, https://www.psychologytoday.com/us/blog/the-athletes-way/201202/the-neuroscience-imagination

of having the mind of a child. Jesus tells us in Matthew 18:3: "Truly I tell you, unless you change and become like little children, you will never enter the kingdom of heaven." Who but a child can believe a human can be born to a virgin, suffer, die, and be buried and then three days later get up from the dead and have lunch with some friends? It makes no logical sense.

And now you get to do this with other aspects of your life in lieu of worry and unrest. Worry is fostered in the imagination. If you are afraid of needles and you get a bronchial infection, you worry about having to get a shot. You haven't had the shot yet, but you imagine having to get one and have preemptive fears about the process. You are imagining the process, and it causes physical reactions to the imagery.

In the What If Wow scenario, you imagine the doctor saying, "A shot is not necessary. You can beat this infection with a quick round of antibiotics." You may argue, "This doesn't prepare me for a shot?" And my argument is this: you can't adequately prepare for pain. If you have ever been in the midst of a dying loved one, you know they are about to pass, and no matter how much you imagine the final moments, the real experience is completely different. The reality is stark and overwhelming. Furthermore, in those last moments, do you want to experience them in life or do you want to be just as devastated and overcome with worry prior to their departure?

You get to decide.

In that decision, you can create more cognizant, precious, and present memories to go with you after they are gone. I speak from experience when I say that this is a more pleasant encounter with life and death. Yes, we are talking about faith. And faith is the substance of things hoped for, the evidence of that not yet seen (Hebrews 11:1). But the reality is *your faith was born as believable in your imagination.* You were told the story of a human born to a virgin; that He suffered, died, was buried; and then three days later He rose from the dead. You had to imagine that to make it your reality, because you were not there to witness it.

You are already using your imagination when you worry and practice What If Ugh. Implementing What If Wow is the invitation to flip the switch and expect to see and experience better and relieve yourself of worry and unrest. And this is the greatest benefit of What If Wow. This is the brain space where you start to operate from inspiration instead of worry and strife. In this space, your mind will be privy to opportunities that are the birthright of the beloved believers, the promises of Christ (John 16:33).

When you are rehashing worst-case scenarios or What If Ugh based on the past, you are not experiencing the unlimited possibilities of a future God planned for you (Jeremiah 29:11).

This is exciting and good news!

The habitual practice of unrest is keeping us from progressing because we are stuck in memory replay of past experiences or past imagined memories instead of creating new hopes and believing in the best God has outlined for us.

Another obstacle in this is that we are told to "grow

up" and that daydreaming of better is coveting. I am not asking you to daydream that you could have your best friend's husband. Yes, that would be coveting and sinful. But if you are worried that your husband is about to lose his job, you are creating images that haven't happened yet, and they are worrisome and unrestful. If you are imagining them and playing them out, your subconscious thinks *that happened*! It has every reason to worry!

I am inviting you to imagine best-case scenarios to experience rest and witness a greater display of faith. The faithful are invited to the practice of believing in the unseen. Prior to the revelation of What If Wow, this evaded me. My limiting beliefs kept me trapped in worry. I knew the worst-case scenario, so that was the mind movie I watched and entertained.

Certainly, all of us have been awakened from a dream and thought, "I am glad I am the only witness to that madness." Dreams can be delightful, terrifying, and comical. I actually think dreams are the mind's playground. It's as if the brain says, "Oh, thank goodness, she's asleep. Now we can do what we want!" As tricky as we have determined it can be to change the mind, the mind can also be easily swayed into thinking something you dreamed or imagined has already happened.

The technique of imagery or visualization has become widely used in elite sports psychology. Olympic athletes use it as a part of their training. They write scripts to help them visualize the perfect performance. In the 1960s, Alan Richardson conducted a study on the power of visualization on basketball free throws. Study participants were divided into three groups. Group A physically practiced free throws for thirty days. Group B mentally visualized successful free throws for thirty days. Group C did not practice and did not visualize.

At the end of the study, as predicted, the group that did not practice or visualize showed no improvements. The group that physically practiced every day showed a 24 percent improvement. And even more exciting, the group that mentally visualized successful free throws improved by 23 percent! Visualization was nearly as effective as physically throwing free throws.[8] Isn't that crazy?

I am certain that Peter never thought he would need to practice believing he could walk on water. And I am convinced that his subconscious, what he knew to be true and safe, was in the habitual practice of doubt. Every time he witnessed Jesus perform a miracle, he became more convinced of Jesus' abilities. At the same time, he was dealing with what he knew, and his deep beliefs most likely continually nagged at him: "Did that really just happen? Maybe the leper was just faking those skin lesions."

I think we are all guilty of this. We hear or experience something outer limits and are quick to say, "Well, I mean maybe it was that greasy burger I had for lunch?" I know this was true of me.

Recently, while driving to the grocery store, I happened to look at my dashboard clock. I noticed it was 12:01 p.m. and instantly heard or thought "Pray for

8 Darleen Barnard, "The Power of Mindset on Sports Performance," Sportsmd.com, April 4, 2019, https://www.sportsmd.com/2019/04/04/the-power-of-mind-set-on-sports-performance/

Kristen." So, I took a moment to say a prayer out loud for my friend in Tennessee. Later that day, I told my other friend Katie about it. The next day Katie sent me a screenshot of Kristen's Instagram post. At the exact moment I had the thought "Pray for Kristen," she was in labor with her baby and experiencing some complications.

What was my response?

"I am sure it was just a coincidence."

Our subconscious doesn't want to navigate off the path of reality unless it is in dream or play mode. It wants and needs to make sense of the situation and deals in what it knows or understands. My conscious mind was thrilled at the idea of being called upon to pray for a sister in Christ. The subconscious mind gives the suggestion "That wasn't real" or "It is just a coincidence." Let's look at this from another point of view. Say you read this line: You can lose ten pounds in ten days by drinking a gallon of water a day.

Your conscious mind sees that information and says, "Okay, I am going to do that." If you read further, you see another sentence that says "You *cannot* lose ten pounds in ten days just by drinking water. It is just water weight. It isn't real weight loss."

You decide to try it anyway, but every time you run to the bathroom, the subconscious says, "This is miserable. I'm not comfortable. I want a soda. How many things are you going to keep trying to change? It didn't work before. You won't stick with this." This is just the subconscious recalling things from the depths of memory and what it knows to keep you in the same place.

We can use thoughts and feelings to convince the subconscious it is wrong about something. Yes, I will back that up with scripture. . .as a man thinketh, so he is (Proverbs 23:7). When you start saying, I can lose ten pounds drinking a gallon of water a day," the subconscious will argue with you, "Nuh-uh!"

To which you retort, "Uh-huh!"

And then you feed it images of success and feel the feeling of having succeeded. You intentionally imagine yourself in a smaller size. When you run to the bathroom, you say, "Wow! I'm so glad this weight is just falling right off me!" You tell a new story to the subconscious, and it cannot tell the difference between reality and imagery. It just knows you feel happy and excited by your newfound experience and success.

When cancer patients go through chemo, doctors recommend imagery to advance healing. They usually recommend that the patient imagine the medicine going into their body like little Pac-Men eating away at the cancer.[9]

So, when it comes to worry and living as a rested, beloved child of God, a child of noble birth, the subconscious is the one that is reminding you of reality. When you first start saying "I am" statements, the subconscious mind is the prosecuting attorney.

Conscious: I am thankful.

Subconscious: For what? You don't have the new

9 Joanne Verkuilen, "The Power of the Mind Can Help Heal Cancer," Thrive Global, June 19, 2018, https://thriveglobal.com/stories/the-science-behind-guided-imagery-how-does-it-work/

clothes you need for work?

Conscious: I am well cared for.

Subconscious: How's that? Where are your new clothes?

Conscious: I am of noble birth.

Subconscious: Your water heater is leaking again . . . *PRINCESS.*

You take a hot minute and imagine better. Use the gift of your amazing brain to tell a new story, organize your thoughts, and change your mind. Look at clothes you need for work on Pinterest, or put a new water heater in an online shopping cart. Then get still and imagine the water heater being delivered. Imagine getting dressed for work in that outfit. Imagine running your fingers over the silky sleeve. *Feel* gratitude and give thanks you have been answered. Believe as if you have received.

Before you fall asleep and your subconscious takes you to lunch with Abraham Lincoln and Elmo, intentionally run feel-good, believing, and faithful scenarios through your mind. Recite some "I am" statements. That sinking Peter mind-set is going to start believing you have already received, and it is going to stop interfering in the belief you have been asked to have! Suddenly, the entire system is working together with great faith.

And there you have it; you are witnessing the impossible. Miracles happen, scenarios you couldn't make up are abundant, and now you can testify with confidence of your rest. Did I mention I love this?

When we operate from memory alone, we shut off the flow of a creative new way. When our minds are organized and we are deciding with God, we operate from divine inspiration. We experience more of God's good will because we are not hosting a party for the negative ways of darkness. We are deciding with God, and He's never wrong. And there is no dreary unrest. Where there is light, there can be no darkness (1 John 1:5).

When I was operating from memory and facts, I was void of His creative ways to save. When I took my thoughts captive and focused on gratitude and love, I received the idea to sell my car. As the money from the sale of the car began to dwindle, I continued the practice. Believing more funds and more opportunities were coming allowed me to continue to stay at rest. Before I knew it, a refund check was in the mail from our car insurance provider, which accrued more faith and belief. Before I knew it, I was picking up my new-to-me little red Beetle. A full cash purchase. No worries. Beep beep.

Think about this: getting lost in thought is nearly a daily occurrence. Have you ever been driving somewhere and arrived with no memory of the trip? How much more enjoyable would it be to be lost in good thoughts rather than bad ones? And while you are only responsible for you, you can still guide others in this newfound freedom by offering them a better line of thinking. Say your best friend calls you distraught and says, "What if my son fails this test and cannot get into college?" You retort, "What if he passes?"

This way of living and thinking will have a ripple effect that I believe could change the lives of many believers and set captives free. By practicing two key concepts—(1) gratitude and (2) love—you can experience real rest too.

Although I am an author, I cannot convey how an organized brain and inspired action changed my life.

In a state of worry and unrest, stop and take negative thoughts captive to experience the clarity of divine inspiration. When you are too tired or scared to create What If Wow scenarios, I recommend a Love Blitz. A Love Blitz is listing as many things as you can think of out loud or on paper that you love. Just as with gratitude, the subconscious will recognize things you love as safe and good. It will respond accordingly. It is a fast change that will become a quick habit to help you reboot.

Let's revisit Philippians 4:8 again: "Finally, brothers and sisters, whatever is true, whatever is noble, whatever is right, whatever is pure, whatever is lovely, whatever is admirable—if anything is excellent or praiseworthy—think about such things." And we're also told to "give thanks in all circumstances; for this is God's will for you in Christ Jesus" (1 Thessalonians 5:18). *God's will for us is to give thanks!*

Our Creator knew that we would respond positively to this, because He created us to live in the abundance of peace and rest! We see this in Colossians 3:15: "Let the peace of Christ rule in your hearts, since as members of one body you were called to peace. And be thankful." Weeks ago, after a very hard day, I had run out of What If Wows and was just done. Overall, things were the pits. I slipped into a hot bath and let loose and wept. Instantly, I had the thought, "Love Blitz." A Love Blitz is a little different from a Gratitude Shift because it is just flooding the mind with the things you love, whether you possess them or not. The things we love and are attracted to are often easier to list, and the mind has their good feeling properties memorized.

But honestly, it had been such a lousy day, I struggled to think of a single thing; then, in an instant, I was flooded with everything in the present moment I loved.

I love cobalt blue.

I love a hot bath.

I love new pajamas.

I love wedding cake.

On and on I went, until. . .I was crying again as my cup was overflowing with gratitude and love. And it was then, naked and sobbing, I heard the stanza for the first line of a children's book idea. I leapt from the tub, barely dried and dressed, and ran to my office. In the clutter of mind, clutter of unrest, and a long day, I was firing on instincts and fight-or-flight responses. I was worn out and sad. But in the throes of a mind like Christ's, I received one of my best ideas to date.

My grandpa once said, "You can't ride two horses with one butt. Ride one horse and do it well." Get on the gratitude pony and give thanks for everything you love, then lean back and be inspired. Everything else will fall into place when love is the driving force. Of course, I am not trying to wear you out with techniques. You need not use all of them. The Gratitude Shift might work just fine or the Love Blitz may be your jam. But the more tools in your belt, the easier the job.

This means you are not a worrier. You are His

beloved. Say it if you don't want a front-row seat to worry. The greatest mystery, Christ in us, the hope of glory (Colossians 1:27), means that we don't have to live in anything other than freedom. Again, the outside world is brutal; we have established that. You may be faced with a horrific situation and don't know what choice to make. But when your mind is in panic mode, restlessly bouncing worst-case scenarios around, you will be deciding from the seat of fear. When you calm the subconscious by *feeling good* about the things you love and give thanks, you will be inspired. You get to decide what your reactions are. You can choose to react with the love of Jesus.

I am not bragging. . .maybe I am. . .but this has brought me to rest. The only hard aspect of uncovering these truths and walking in this freedom is I want it for everyone. While I have much more freedom to talk about and many more words to write, I don't get to decide who reads them or if they will implement them. Lucky for me, I don't have to worry about that.

REST, GIRL REFLECTION

When we operate from the space of an organized brain, one that is synced with the singular thought of Christ, we will meet with rest. It will be our natural state of being.

DREAM JOURNALING

Recount a time when you were inspired by an idea. What was going on in your life? Were you in a season of rest or a season of stress?

Chapter Sixteen

NEVER LOST GIRL

He has said, "I will never leave you nor forsake you."
HEBREWS 13:5 ESV

Obviously, I have been on a wild ride in my belief. And while there are plenty of scriptures to back up my newfound hope, the words *I told you so* have been rattling around in my head. After I finally deciphered them, I found even more rest.

As of late, I have had some huge prayers answered. And I don't suspect, I know for sure, the next few months will play out like a movie in the story of my life. How do I know? Well, because God told me so.

No, I am not taking any experimental drugs. I can't say that "I told you so" is audible, but I can't say it isn't. It has advanced me in my faith. And not the nod and kneel and make Sunday lunch kind of belief. Real, tangible, uninhibited belief. Suddenly I picture myself spinning in a field of wildflowers, completely free and peace filled, blond curls blowing in the wind, and dressed in a humanely sourced or upcycled sundress with daisies in my hair.

At the core of this freedom is the understanding of my belief in terms of calling it done. What I continue to uncover is that at the root of unrest is the doubt of the heart (subconscious). You can say, "I believe," with your mouth (a conscious decision). Maggie, John, Luke, Sophie, Sam, and Charlie are my children. I can tell you this. But you might look at a few of them and say, "They don't look a thing like you." I could argue they are mine and still not be able to convince you. But in my heart, you could never, ever convince me they are not my children.

This is the substance of my motherhood. I told you they are my children. But I know for a fact this is the truth. And faith is the substance of things hoped for, evidence of that not seen. God says, "I told you so. I told you this would be what counts you righteous. And I also told you, you need only believe."

But what we profess with our mouths is different from what we know in our hearts. This is where "I told you so" comes into play. In Mark 11:24, Jesus says, "Therefore I tell you, whatever you ask for in prayer, believe that you have received it, and it will be yours."

As I have proposed before, I have asked, but then I go to work on my unbelief. I never stop to believe that what I asked for has already been received. I further propose this is at the root of our unrest. The place where we are left wondering, "Wait a minute, I asked in His name and He totally left me hanging!" Then, to make myself feel warm and fuzzy again, I say, "Well! I guess He is just in a different time zone than me!" Or worse, "That must not have been His will."

His will is going to get done; He is God. But my wants and needs are not a shot in the dark when I decide with Him. This is the dance of always being with Him and experiencing true rest.

As we advance in the practices of rest, our words and feelings are key players in the equation. However, I know you want to see some proof, and so I am here to offer you a penny for your thoughts.

How many pennies on the sidewalk do you suppose you have walked past, never noticing them? Probably a bunch. The value of a penny is, well, a penny. Our deep belief is "It's just a penny." You can't even get a gumball for a penny anymore.

So here is a fun practice: I want you to look for a penny on the road or even around your house. If you want, you can pray for a random penny or say into the mirror, "I am on the hunt for a penny!" Look at a penny and say, "I love pennies. I love finding pennies. I hope I find a penny today!" Then, as soon as you find a penny, I want you to get excited—like over the top, like a child who finds a penny. You know how a kid acts when they find a coin; they act like they just won the lottery. I want you to use your conscious mind to relay the message to the RAS to start letting pennies through to the subconscious as a great thing.

"I found a penny! I am so thankful I found this penny! I want to find a lot of pennies! The more pennies I have . . . the more I can put in the collection plate for the food drive! Praise God for this penny!" Examine the penny. Read the penny. It has an important statement on it, one that means something to you—*In God We Trust*. Rub the penny. Close your eyes and think about the penny. Say it again: "I want to find pennies. I love finding pennies!" In good time, you are going to be spying pennies like a hawk spies bunnies in a field. It is no longer just a penny; it has value to the RAS!

I understand you might be thinking, "It is still just a penny! I have bigger issues causing me unrest." But what I am demonstrating to you here is that you can change your mind. Let's go back to Peter walking on the water. Peter was a fisherman. His RAS and subconscious knew how water worked. But Peter was able to walk on the water because of a miracle. Peter's love for and belief in Jesus made it possible. But when he saw the wind, alarm bells went off from his RAS to his brain and alerted him to the possibility of drowning. Experience told him that this was impossible. And he began to sink.

Granted, he had been hanging out with Jesus, the One and only. He had seen Jesus perform other miracles. Again, this is a testament to how difficult it can be to overcome limiting beliefs. But just like all biblical inspiration, we can use this incident to advance our faith. Out of our mouths we say we believe, but pesky experience reminds us, "It didn't work out before. Why would it now?" Or with our mouths we might pray, "I need that promotion. . ." But pesky experience might say, "When I was little and my dad got that big promotion, our family fell apart. I better just stay in my old position," or "I didn't get it last time. I don't have what it takes to do that job. I am not as qualified as Sheila."

When we can get our subconscious in line with our conscious mind, we are able to experience a deeper level of belief. The kind that believes we will be answered. And no, this is not magic, and it is not the miracle. But think about this: we are not accustomed to seeing miracles or abundance. We work in reality.

A penny is just a penny.

This exercise is a stepping-stone in the practice of changing our minds. Our minds are more readily changed through *feeling* experiences. If you feel the thrill, if you give thanks, smile, laugh, or talk about how wonderful it was to find a penny, the RAS will start notifying the subconscious, "Wow! She really likes pennies. They make her feel happy."

So how would this apply with the promotion I mentioned above? If out of my mouth I pray, "God, I really need that promotion," then I can change my mind and feed the RAS affirming thoughts about the promotion.

Writing out prayers, wants, and don't wants is an excellent way to do this. You feel the pen in your hand, and touch is another way to activate the RAS. For example, You write,

> *God, I really need that promotion. I fear that it will negatively affect my family. I know Sheila has more education than I do. But I am really good at long-term projects. I am a people person, and I enjoy meeting the other project managers. Open my eyes to ways I can better increase my relationship with my family. Show me how to present myself and my abilities with*

efficiency and confidence. I believe that You are looking out for me. I trust that if this promotion isn't what is best, You will show me other ways to advance. Amen.

Then I can pick positives to start saying out loud (I recommend doing this in front of the mirror) so the RAS sees and hears the affirmations coming from you.

1. I am the perfect candidate for this job.
2. I am a good parent and spouse.
3. I manage my time well.
4. I am really good at long-term projects.
5. I work well with project managers.
6. I am a people person.
7. I spy opportunities all around me.
8. I believe in miracles.
9. I trust God.

When the RAS is notifying the subconscious of positives, you will see and experience more opportunities to meet your goals. In the opposite way, if you are saying, "God, I really need that promotion. I probably won't get it. I am not qualified. I am worried my family will fall apart. But, gosh, I need Your help," then you call your sister, ask her to pray, and then talk about how it probably won't happen. And when the RAS notifies the subconscious to see more evidence, it won't happen. The belief is not in an ability to walk on water; it is drowning in disbelief and worry.

What I am suggesting has a human element. If you are afraid and worried, your overall demeanor and chemistry project a lack of confidence and charisma. Your senses are keen to the only evidence you know and understand. On the spiritual side, these limiting beliefs convey to God the opposite of what you are asking. He is a good Father who wants to care for you. So that prayer might be met with the answer, "My girl isn't ready to have that promotion. She is so afraid for her family. She is so intimidated by Sheila. She needs some more time to prepare for this job."

Now the penny exercise is a method of changing your mind about something we know to be small so that we can move on to believing even bigger—and rest. This can be the proof in the pudding. I would also like to give you a little more evidence. I used cars earlier, but do you have a "thing"? My friend always sees the number 717, her anniversary. Prior to learning about the RAS, I was always amazed how often and where she would see it. But now I get it. The RAS is alerting her to this number because it means something important to her!

Oh, my goodness, we are such interesting creations.

This exercise is going to give you some concrete evidence that by *feeling* something new, you can get your subconscious in line with your words. Feelings convey new messages about your deep beliefs, and then suddenly you are going to not only spy pennies, you are going to recognize when the prayers of your mouth are not in line with the prayers of your heart.

A few weeks after I learned about the RAS, it occurred to me how many messages I have fed my mind and made their characteristics part of my character. The lie that stuck out was the "lie" that I constantly lose things. From car keys to sunglasses, phone chargers to my wallet, I used to misplace things dozens of times a day. This kept me frazzled and unrested. However, the RAS conveyed the message to my subconscious, "She's doing her thing!" Losing things was my thing because I said it was.

So, I began saying, "I never lose anything. I am organized, efficient, and rested." Within about two weeks, I was able to prove to my RAS and subconscious that these things *were* true of me. Furthermore, I experience the real feelings of that accomplishment. After thousands of hours spent hunting for my car keys, knowing they are right where I left them, and I remember where that is, I am flooded with the joy of truly being "organized, efficient, and rested."

How many times have you heard someone or yourself say, "I looked for it for over an hour, and it was right in front of me the whole time!" I have said it many times. I recognize this is the RAS and subconscious's game of hide-and-seek. But those parts of your brain only continue to play the game when they believe this is a necessary routine in your game of life.

Say you are always late. Guess what? Say you can't meet the right guy? Yep. Say that you are a terrible communicator, unsuccessful, afraid, bitter, or "sick to death of. . ." and you know what you are? Those things.

About three years ago, my mom gave me an adorable hard-shell sunglasses case. I think I had it in my possession for all of three days before I lost it. I gave myself a little break; we had just moved, and I was launching my first book. Basically, I was doing the best I could with the brain I had trained. Three weeks ago, my mom, daughter, and I were making a quick trip to Vegas. I was out shopping for a new outfit for the trip when I spotted a similar sunglasses case. I had the thought, "I am going to replace the one I lost." Almost instantly, an image flashed in my mind of a shelf by our back door, and on it was my "lost" sunglasses case. I rushed home.

The moment I walked in the back door, I spotted it. Just about eye level, in full view, was the case I had deemed "lost." That shelf and the case were dusty. I mean, out of sight out of mind. But it was clearly in sight. With my conscious mind, I had deemed it lost, and I took no aggressive actions or desperate feelings to find it. So, the RAS saw no reason to alert my subconscious to show it to me. When I saw the similar case at the clothing store, I felt the need to buy it because mine was *lost*. It was then the RAS nudged the subconscious, "She doesn't lose things. Remind her where it is."

Game over.

Granted, while losing our keys is a frustrating process, think about the bigger things that are holding you in a state of constant unrest. Here is where I will tread lightly: I know that this all seems pretty easy from a gal who has been practicing it for a while and who got pregnant at the drop of a hat. There are women who desperately want a baby. I am not making light of this painful struggle. But I want to use an example that is nearly cliché. How many stories have been told about infertility and adoption? Say a couple struggles with infertility and secondary infertility for years. Finally, when it looks like there is no way they can conceive, they adopt a baby. . .and end up pregnant a month later.

When we look at this aspect of conception in conjunction with the brain and body, what is the reason behind this phenomenon? This is my hypothesis. A woman is stressed and heartbroken over her inability to conceive. She professes her lack; she laments her want. Maybe she prays, "God, please. . .let me have a baby." There are doctor visits, shots, pills, procedures, and more angst. Baby showers nearly break her, and she steers clear of the diaper and formula aisle at Target. At lunch with a friend, she breaks into tears with the statement, "*I am infertile.*"

Her subconscious says, "Right, this is infertility. It doesn't feel good, but I know what to expect." Then she is handed her adopted newborn. She's finally a mother. Everything she had hoped to be since the first time she picked up a baby doll. And those feelings and the emptiness she has known as "infertile" send a new message to the subconscious. "Babies make her happy. Being a mother is a great situation for her! She should have a baby!"

Please hear me when I say this is not always the case. But also hear me when I say that it is a good example of staying in a place of unrest. The hard part of the example is this: there are some situations where we are entirely lost in our lack, and the very brain we house is running the show, undoing our need through the ritual of practicing what it thinks is what we want, what it believes is a safe place.

It was not easy for me to use the example above. I never want to hurt anyone. I have miscarried. And I have said goodbye to a child that I mothered for two years. There are labels that I have written beneath my name and next to it that in some ways describe me. But they are not the entirety of me. What I want for you, for the world, is peace and rest. Knowing that there is a battle helps us be battle ready. Having the right weapons allows us to fight back. Holding the faith when all is lost, well, that is the winning blow.

Our hurts, struggles, and losses are not what we are called to proclaim; our victory is. As my friend and editor, Katie, ran through this chapter, we both winced. And yet, sometimes the hard things must be said. Your Instagram handle @foreverinfertile or @cancersucks speaks to the subconscious, and the subconscious claims it as its own.

There is a connection between our body, mind, and soul. God created each of us in a beautiful, intricate design (Psalm 139:13–18). So, when we experience rest in one of these areas, it impacts the others, and the opposite is true as well. When we prescribe to defeat and a restless existence, that is what we are on the lookout for and that is what we experience. But you can be clothed in love—fear doesn't have to dictate your next steps.

Colossians 3:14–17 (NLT) says,

> *Above all, clothe yourselves with love, which binds us all together in perfect harmony. And let the peace that comes from Christ rule in your hearts. For as members of one body you are called to live in peace. And always be thankful. Let the message about Christ, in all*

its richness, fill your lives. Teach and counsel each other with all the wisdom he gives. Sing psalms and hymns and spiritual songs to God with thankful hearts. And whatever you do or say, do it as a representative of the Lord Jesus, giving thanks through him to God the Father.

Put on love, be cloaked in peace, exude thanks—not because you're out of touch with reality but because you are in touch with the One who wove you together and wrote redemption, restoration, and new life into the story—yours included.

You are strong. You are brave. You are a warrior. Those triumphant words are pleading with you, "Claim me." Mother Teresa once said, "I will never attend an anti-war rally; if you have a peace rally, invite me."[10] What we speak, rise against, and proclaim as our identity becomes our identity.

Yes, we need our babies to be safe, and drunk drivers need to get off the road. Oh my, do whatever is medically possible to be healed or have that baby. But I pray that struggle isn't the thing you cling to rather than the triumph of His redemption. We are created with passion for a purpose. And the battle has been won. We proclaim in Jesus' name that it is on earth as it is in heaven. That is our battle cry, and when we believe it, we will live it.

Snoozin' baby love.

REST, GIRL REFLECTION

You are never outside of the safety of God's love. He

10 Mother Teresa, Goodreads, accessed February 14, 2021, https://www.goodreads.com/quotes/859052-i-will-never-attend-an-anti-war-rally-if-you-have

made no plans for you to cause you harm. While you may walk through the valley of the shadow of death, He will be right beside you. He is the way, the truth, and the life.

DREAM JOURNALING

Can you recount a time when God mystified you? Can you now see why?

Chapter Seventeen

BETTER TOGETHER

Then make my joy complete by being like-minded, having the same love, being one in spirit and of one mind.
PHILIPPIANS 2:2

Thirty-some odd years ago, back in the days when I deemed myself dingy and a loser of all things, I worked at a clothing store in the mall. It was the norm for me to call my dad, crying to report my car had been stolen. It hadn't. I didn't even want that car, why would a car thief? No, it wasn't stolen. I had just lost it. Again.

The car of my youth was a brown 1980s Toyota Corona. The body style was a mix between an old BMW and a Lincoln Town Car. It was the color of poo. The radio was held in place with duct tape, a Tears for Fears fan club sticker, and a wad of watermelon Hubba Bubba. To add to "Wanda's" charm, the exterior driver's side door handle was missing. When I came out of work, assuming I could find the car, I had to unlock my car from the passenger side and either climb over the passenger seat to the driver's side or reach across and open the driver's side door and walk back around to the other side to get in.

One day I arrived at work, parked, got out of my car, and was met with an inferno blast of hot, ninety mph, West Texas whirlwind. The wind blew my waist-length hair back and simultaneously forced the car door shut. To my horror, my long locks were shut in the door with no handle. Left with no options, all of them leaving me vulnerable, I had to yell for help. A man in the parking lot several rows over heard me and ran to my aid.

"What's wrong?" he asked.

"My hair is caught in my car door."

Confused, he said, "Just open it?"

Humiliated, I answered, "I can't. There's no handle on the driver's side. Will you take my keys and unlock the passenger side door and open it from inside?" He did, and I thanked him and went on my way.

Other than the ridiculousness of this tale, I am sure you're wondering what it has to do with rest. I have a point. Sometimes we get stuck—trapped in a place that is not safe, healthy, or well. Sometimes we get in that situation by our own folly. Yet always there is help. We were promised a Helper (John 14:26).

Real help doesn't leave the mop floating in the bucket of dirty water. Real help doesn't jack up the car, take off the tire, and leave you standing by the side of the road with no spare. Real help doesn't propose to deliver freedom and rest and wake you up from a dead sleep to tell you that you are six months behind on your mortgage payment.

Real help delivers.

Real help was sent. Do we acknowledge that help? Or are we in the habitual practice of believing we must chase help and that the help is the same kind of help that humans offer, which is never the complete help.

My brother-in-law always says, "That was the opposite of help." And the opposite of help is to focus on that which is of no help at all. As a mom of many, if I had a quarter for every time I said, "Never mind! I will just do it myself!" I would be extremely wealthy.

The "do it myself" aspect of this is that I know how to mop better than an eleven-year-old. They are not real help. But in the realm of the Holy Spirit, the help is real. He knows how to do it better, and He finishes what He starts. The mop bucket is emptied, rinsed out, dried, and put back in the pantry where it belongs.

At my best, I am so enthralled with this help that I do not stumble, and none of the arrows or ways of the world are for me. I am rescued, safe, and have been helped and continue to embrace that help. There is no opposite.

Yesterday, Justin, Sam, and Charlie came to Galveston Island to see me at my writer's escape. They played in the ocean and I organized words. This morning, Sam and I went to the laundry on the first floor of the hotel to wash their sandy swimsuits. Things in Galveston are humming. It's the weekend and there's a biker event going on. The hotel is full, as is everything on the island, including the elevators.

Sam and I waited an unusually long time for the elevator. When the doors finally opened, we were met with a verbal assault. As we stepped toward the doors, an older man, barely a foot taller than Sam, barked, "Nuh-uh! You aren't getting on this elevator with your nose hanging out of your face mask!" I was shocked and looked down at Sam, whose mask had slipped down beneath his nose. I put my hand on Sam's chest and stepped back and said, "We'll wait for the next elevator." The man shook his head in visible disgust, and as the door shut, I heard him say to the women next to him, "Idiots! There is a pandemic, and they are too stupid to. . ."

He disappeared from sight. We waited a beat before we pushed the button to activate a new ride down. Writing this out, I would note the stairs wouldn't have killed us.

Fear or love?

For the loyal fans of Sam-I-am, I know, I was offended too. He is just a little boy. His "boneless" little nose doesn't hold his Baby Yoda medical mask perfectly in place. As a wordsmith, there are things I could say. I could have posted a picture of my sweet boy, his button nose peeking out of the mask, which I agree offers no real protection from the virus.

Thousands of followers would join me in my offense and rally to Sam's defense. The behavior we encountered was harsh and alarming. And with the voices in my head, organized and in unison with the help that is the Holy Spirit, I chose love. I will tell you what I told Sam.

That reaction was not kind, and it was generated from fear. Being afraid is fretful and no fun. The ugliness was a bit much, but we cannot know what that man faced in the masked face of Covid. Perhaps he or his companions were high risk; perhaps they were just mean. Either way, I chose love. I explained this to Sam, but he was either oblivious or delirious from dehydration. Still, we have a choice when we are scared or offended or anything in between. Love or fear.

It isn't that I'm not tempted to be offended. But as my friend Adam says, "Offense is a choice." So, with the help of the Holy Spirit, I chose not to be offended.

After we finished with the laundry, we were back on the elevator, masks securely in place. This time we were met with a huge biker dude. He had to have been at least six foot six. His beard hung to his waist, he was dressed in leather and chains, and he was covered in menacing, nearly threatening tattoos, including one of a skull and crossbones on his *unmasked* face. The wall of a man looked at Sam and said, "Hey, little guy! Are you going to the beach?" And Sam said, "No sir, I have a stomachache." The man said, "I hope your mommy knows those masks are just a hoax to keep Americans paranoid and under the thumb of the man." The doors opened, and the couple stepped out of the elevator.

I am a little chilled by the clash and the opportunity, toward the end of this book, to have met with such stark contrasts. It is not that I have run out of things to say about a life of rest. But I am undone by how God has allowed me to continue to see the truth even on a break from writing on the way to wash some shorts.

My help comes from the Lord. I am better with Him. Were my opinion needed here, I could tell you what a jerk the first guy was. All of us are doing our best.

Masks slip, they get left in the car, and in South Texas, where it is unseasonably warm and humid, they are not comfortable. The second guy, well, I would not say this to his face, but come on, man. All of us are doing our best. We are simply trying to follow the rules and get by the best we know how.

Currently, our Marine-baby son and bride have COVID-19. We have lost friends and have come very close to losing others. What we have faced as citizens of the world has been scary. And even when we are scared, we are given the choice: fear or love?

My son and his wife would tell you Covid is real and no fun. My publicist, who has been unable to hug her daddy and has talked to him through a window screen at his retirement home for eleven months, would say, "Please cover your face."

We could banter back and forth. The looming question: Would elevator guy #1 have been so brazen with elevator guy #2? Because that would have been a sight to see.

But really, there are only two choices. You know them, and I will say them again: fear or love? While elevator guy #2 might profess he is not afraid of anything, the fact is a profession against the face mask and the rules of the hotel where we are staying is a profession made in fear. Fear of being wrong, controlled, or appearing weak might appear to be a tough stance against "the man," but it is simultaneously a feeble attempt at hiding how very afraid he really is.

As a society, we would be better if we all worked together in love. I know that is not always possible.

We choose division in our actions and verbiage. Those darned Democrats, the dang Republicans, mask wearers, and mask defiers—we habitually pick camps, set up our tents, and collect our offenses.

From this space we are isolated by our contempt and defined by our stance. I have been an active participant in the folly. What I remember about this campground was exhaustion. Election results, polls, opinions, fake news, real news, and the uprising that followed are not the lullaby of the great help we were promised.

I know myself pretty well. The post I could have written about elevator guy #1 would have been quite brilliant. I mean, I love Jesus. . .and you aren't going to want to yell at my kid. But together with the Holy Spirit, who always chooses love, I was left at rest.

The Holy Spirit sees what we cannot. When we are in tune with Him, we get a glimpse of His vision. In our best Christianese, we might say it was an attack from the enemy or a sinful nature. With our experience, we might just say it was political division. With the Holy Spirit, we know, Jesus died for that too.

There are times that we are called to action, response, and correction. But barking my opinions to decided minds or verbally assaulting those with whom I do not agree is not my job. Sitting in a mud puddle is no help. And swimming in a sea of tranquility doesn't hurt a thing. As a writer, I want my words to matter. They will for some and not so much for others. But while I don't have to be wronged, He is always right. His ways are perfect, and He offered to carry my burdens with strong, capable efficiency (Matthew 11:30).

I reread a post I wrote years ago. I am not that girl anymore. She was witty, and her words and wording are familiar. But she was also a creature of unrest. She made feeble attempts, trying to fix the world one blog post at a time in the vast, unruly rage of the internet.

This scripture from Matthew 6:33 (KJV) comes to mind: "Seek ye first the kingdom of God, and His righteousness; and all these things shall be added unto you." When I seek Him above all else, His righteousness is my righteousness, and His rest is added unto me.

This includes human companionship that's meant to help as well. There is something good and right to be said about setting a tent up in the camp of like-minded. Here is where we must be cloaked in the love of the Helper in guiding us in our human relationships. I imagine that I could have waited on the good Lord to send another blast of wind to magically open my old Toyota's door, freeing me and my blond locks from the snare. Alas, He sent a trustworthy human.

There are many humans who add to the rest of this life. They bring joy, laughter, comfort, and companionship. God even wanted to share in companionship, otherwise, why would He mess with the nonsense we create? Well, we know, because He thought it was "good" to partner in the experience (Genesis 1:31).

Very often we encounter beings that are life-giving. Very often we encounter beings that are life-sucking. Here is a good time to remind you, you were created for love, joy, peace, forbearance, kindness, goodness, faithfulness, gentleness, and self-control (Galatians 5:22–23). We can expend much energy attempting to make people be who we need them to be. However, it is a much easier road to trust the Helper to handpick people to journey with us who already are exactly who we need. And we do need—I don't know that we can deny that.

At my first writers' conference, I was in a breakout session with other author wannabes. We sat in a circle and gave our "elevator pitches." Just the quickest breakdown for our book idea, should we meet with an agent or acquisitions editor. The ideas and topics varied, but one in particular stood out. An older woman who explained this was her nineteenth conference in the last four years was desperate to find a publisher for the book that "God told her to write." Her elevator pitch was interesting, I'll give her that.

"Clara, a fifteen-year-old Amish girl is kidnapped from her home by a violent motorcycle gang of zombies. She is gang-raped and then used as a decoy while the zombies rob banks. The motor club blazes across the United States, terrorizing citizens. So, in tune with the Lord and strong in her faith walk, Clara prays she will be saved from her living nightmare. . ."

Long story short, there is an end-of-days battle with the zombies and. . .*space aliens*, which the Lord Himself allowed to infiltrate the world to save poor Clara.

I would like to introduce you to the collective consciousness. The collective consciousness is the set of shared beliefs, ideas, and moral attitudes that operate as a unifying force within society. Generally, it does not refer to the specific moral conscience but to a shared understanding of social norms.[11]

The collective conscience in that breakout session is best described as ten speechless wordsmiths. I have yet to see that book in circulation. I met the author again at another convention a couple years later. She was a little saltier, slightly jaded, and a lot more determined. Her belief (subconscious/heart) in the content and storyline were unshakable. And the world and most editors, collectively, dreaded to hear the pitch again.

I hope that she had community. Who am I to say? Maybe it is a brilliant idea. I wonder what my editor at Barbour will have to say? Pipe down, Annie. If you love zombie-Amish-Christian storylines, I bet I can track her down for you.

However, I don't foresee this being a thing.

But our deep beliefs are impacted by the collective consciousness. I can testify to that just by turning on the news. Our beliefs and convictions are greatly impacted by the people around us. We may be talked out of our ideas or talked further into them, depending on the company.

If like attracts like, we will often find ourselves surrounded by people who are a match to our positions. Furthermore, Jesus Himself acknowledged power in numbers: "For where two or three gather in my name, there am I with them" (Matthew 18:20).

Still, especially if we believe we are on a unique mission from God, sometimes that means you must hold vigil alone. If we are not hurting anyone and have the

11 "Collective Consciousness," Wikipedia, last modified February 9, 2021, https://en.wikipedia.org/wiki/Collective_consciousness

purest of motives, He is going to finish what He started and complete the good work He began (Philippians 1:6).

No human can fill us up in the ways we were intended to be filled. In chapter eleven, we classified the belief that there is someone or something that "completes us" as a *Liable Love*. And while we are venturing into new verbiage and beliefs about such things, I know there are some people in my life that sure help me feel a lot more like me.

As I have progressed further into the world of rest, it is most dear to know there are humans in my life that I can count on to remind me who I am and who He is. There are others that I have had to wish well and move away from. But the like minds, the ones that know what is for them and what is not, they are my favorite.

After hours of writing, as I closed in on the end of this book, I decided to take a break from writing and stroll on the beach in my bare feet. The four-lane boulevard that separates my hotel and the seawall is always pretty busy, but this week it has been intensely congested with droves of motorcycle enthusiasts parading up and down the road. By the skin of my teeth and no tire marks on my hiney, I survived my klutzy bolt to the beachside.

I strolled and prayed. Ideas and more words accompanied me on my walk. My subconscious, privy to the dangers of crossing busy roads in flip-flops, whispered, "*Hey, do you have a master plan for getting back across to the hotel alive*?" This nipped at my sandy heels and begged for a solution. No sooner had I resolved to walk the full mile and a half to the nearest crosswalk, meaning a full mile and a half trek back to the hotel, did I receive a text from a friend. She giddily explained her implementation of praying, asking for something, believing. . . *feeling* with her whole heart as if she had received, and the blessing of the teaching. I bantered back, I AM SO GLAD. PUT THAT ON MY TOMBSTONE IF I AM SQUASHED BY A HARLEY ON MY WAY BACK TO THE HOTEL.

What can I say? Even fifty-eight thousand words later, the mind is a hard nut to crack.

She texted, WHO IS THIS? WHERE IS MY FRIEND WHO ASKS, BELIEVING SHE IS SAFE AND WELL? I sat down on a rock, just shy of the incoming tide, and asked, "Hey, Jesus, I need safe space to cross the street. Would you please tell me when it is safe to head back?"

I sat and watched the waves come and go. I pictured myself leisurely crossing the road, free from worry, blissfully safe. I prayed, "Thank You, Jesus, for this blessing. Thank You for surrounding me with wise friends, protective angels, and love. Thank You for the humans in my life who remind me of Your goodness."

And still I sat. . .and then I heard, "Go."

I picked up my flip-flops and water bottle and headed up the seawall stairs to an empty boulevard. I strolled leisurely back to the hotel. There was not a vehicle in sight.

The road to the beach brings me to another point—the enemy. While I do not subscribe to a creepy, crawly, demon roaming the earth looking for humans to strike down and destroy (give me a hot minute, I will explain), I do believe the enemy is fully on board with keeping us laid out and broken, with everything in our heads. This is actually scarier to me. Now, the reason I do not profess a belief in a singular, evil entity wandering in and out of random lives per the description so many Christians may endorse is because:

1. If Satan had that much power, everything would be lost.
2. Where there is light, there is no darkness. And the world is no longer dark because the Light, Jesus, overcame it.
3. Think then on whatever is good, pure, and holy (Philippians 4:8).
4. There are still just two choices: love or fear. Perfect love casts out fear.

A confused mind about God, the devil, his power, darkness, the Old Testament and the New cannot find rest. It is a mind that is desperate to stay in the safety of what it can make sense of. If I hand you a movie on DVD and it has had the last scene edited to the middle and the first is at the end, how well can you explain the plot?

Battling the mind and self with scriptures such as "Nothing in all creation will ever be able to separate us from the love of God" (Romans 8:39 NLT) with the same mind that has memorized "He will tear them down and not build them up" (Psalm 28:5 NASB) leaves the subconscious in a terrorized and confused existence. Exhausting, no?

The accusation that this might meet with is that we must be privy to the enemy's ways (1 Peter 5:8). Yes, we must. And a mind not filled with light is kept in the dark. A dark mind is desperate for light, and so it wanders, lost, afraid, and confused. A mind filled with the truth of Christ, a mind saturated in Christ, in union with the wholeness of who He is. . .

Here is your flashlight and a map home.

God is entirely good. Jesus is the Prince of Peace. There is no rebuttal to Him overcoming the world. The issue I take with imagining a ghastly beast out to get us is that the mind then believes in an incomplete Savior. It creates a Jesus that only kind of saved us. He saved me. . .*but* then He made a monster to destroy me if I don't watch out.

So, I was sitting on the balcony of my hotel typing ninety to nothing. The traffic below was loud and thick with speeding vehicles. Suddenly, horns were blaring and brakes were screeching. I looked and spied a homeless man with a shopping cart mindlessly crossing the street, completely ignoring his impending doom. I was left to conclude that he either had great faith in the law of pedestrians or he just didn't care. Perhaps life was too hard. If he were to be killed by an eighteen-wheeler, so be it.

I do not know anything else about the rogue street crosser except that he made it across alive. What I do know is that crossing the road without safe passage is deadly. After I return home, I will still be aware of the busy Seawall Boulevard in Galveston. But when I recount my experience there, that road will be of no threat to me. So why would that be the focus? How ridiculous would it be for me to blame traffic for every single issue I encounter?

"The painting I tried to sell still hasn't sold. It must

be an attack from the traffic."

"My child is struggling with bullying at school. It must be because of the traffic."

"Work is so much harder with my new grouchy boss. Traffic is really after me."

Knowing that traffic is dangerous is of benefit. Blaming traffic or giving it the verbal power to destroy me from the safety of my second-story office back at home—that is the opposite of rest. Knowing the sneaky snake is dangerous is of benefit. Giving him credit or power from the restful, loving embrace of Jesus is nonsense.

Recently, we were invited to visit a church. I checked out the church's website. This was their statement of faith: *We are an army sent to battle the Enemy. We raise our voices in union and cry out against the wicked and the legion Satan himself has sent to destroy us. We, the faithful, are armed with the power of the cross and will not rest until the Liar is thrown back into hell where he belongs.*

Hard. Pass.

To sit and listen to the powers of darkness in a room full of consciousnesses that believe he is ours to defeat is to sit in the ashes of misery and unrest. That is not from Jesus. If I am getting out of bed and into pantyhose and heels, I want to hear Good News and the Truth of who Christ is. I am fully cognizant of a life without Jesus. If I want to worship in the pew of darkness, well, I can stay in my jammies, watch the news, or troll through Facebook.

Nothing can separate you from His love. Ask, believe as if you have received, and it will be yours. There are only two choices: love or fear. He loves you. No buts. We indeed are better together when every motive is made in the name of love. Even when we are physically alone, He is never more than a whisper away from us.

Everything that is good and restful is always present. We are invited to experience a life of rest, one that is safe from the outside because of what is on the inside.

A perfect place to change our minds not from without. . .but from within.

The best rest of all.

REST, GIRL REFLECTION

Sometimes we get stuck, trapped in a place that is not safe, healthy, or well. Sometimes we get in that situation by our own folly. Yet always there is help. We were promised a Helper. . .and help is here.

DREAM JOURNALING

Who are your humans who are a real help? What is your relationship with the Holy Spirit? Take a moment to write some things you know to be true of the Holy Spirit.

Chapter Eighteen

NOT FROM WITHOUT, FROM WITHIN

Let perseverance finish its work so that you may be mature and complete, not lacking anything.

JAMES 1:4

Sometime in September 2020, nine months into my journey of rest, I was on a walk in our neighborhood. My mind was bantering some rowdy scenarios; I'm pretty sure they revolved around our ongoing house hunt. In the spirit of candidness, I again admit that I was stressed. Our home is lovely. Still, moving to a house with land is something we as a family want.

This tale doesn't end with a bolt of lightning or the manifestation of a little house on the edge of town, where Justin doesn't have to engage with friendly neighbors. But, recognizing my internal strife, I went into an immediate banter of thanksgiving. I'd already asked God to help us find a house; but circling the mountain of unrest was causing me greater unrest. So, I thanked

God for the impending view, the quiet, and the privacy. I know it is coming. I imagined Justin, Sam, and Charlie fishing in a pond at a yet undisclosed location. And I gave thanks.

My mind began to quiet, and I took a deep, cleansing breath. I filled my lungs with fresh, pine-laced, humid air. Loosening my clenched jaw and tight throat, I felt the welcomed relief of rest.

Feeling His presence and peace, I decided to inquire, "We are ready financially and emotionally, we believe. . . Why is this taking so long? Am I missing something?"

I know, you might be weary of having to hear everything that goes on in my head, but you're still here, so it is not all on me. But this download, although grammatically odd, made perfect sense to me in an instant.

"Not from without, from within."

Over the course of the weeks to come, I heard it again and again. *Not from without, from within.* This chapter has been bubbling up and begging to cut loose. Y'all, *not from without, from within.*

To live without is to focus on all the outside forces that compete with our rest like a jewelry thief in Tiffany's with no security in sight. To live within is to operate with the strength Jesus provides and rest in who He is and who we are in Him. When our conscious and subconscious are collectively in tune with what He has promised and living from the place of belief, everything we stress over, every single thing that causes our pain, unrest, and turmoil, is born from without. Outside of us, from without, our subconscious seeks to find what is not in our physical reach. From without, we are convinced we have not received what we have requested, what we need or want.

But from within, there is *nothing* we are without. Scripture tells us, "Ask and it will be given to you; seek and you will find; knock and the door will be opened to you. For everyone who asks receives; the one who seeks finds; and to the one who knocks, the door will be opened" (Matthew 7:7–8). There is no *but*.

When our eyes are swollen from crying, our hearts are weary from the ache, and our minds are worn from the turmoil, what is it that we need outside of ourselves and He who dwells in us that we are without?

Nothing.

We lack not one single thing.

This was a huge revelation for me; it has advanced my renewed mind exponentially. A mind that is constantly in search of that which will satisfy from the outside is constantly met with the disappointments of lack and tangible realities. But a mind that is (or will be) convinced that it houses the Truth, that within it is the power that creates and provides for every need—Christ in us the hope of glory—is at rest.

From *without*, we lament our need. From *within*, there is no need. In this place of understanding and the belief and *feeling* we are provided for, we are transformed. The subconscious quiets and becomes satisfied because it believes. Just as we were promised, all we have strived to comprehend ceases to be a struggle when finally the door is opened to the power of belief.

I remember years ago, with a van full of small

children, Justin and I took a trip to a distant state park. As we drove through a little town in East Texas, we made a stop to fill our gas tank, empty bladders, change someone's diaper, and buy more cheese crackers to quiet our brood. At the pump next to us was a man decked out in camouflage, filling his diesel pickup. His passenger side door was open, and a little boy, maybe three, dressed in a tiny camo ensemble, stood on the seat pretending to drive the truck. The little boy chatted about "huntin' wif Daddy."

Busy wrangling our own children, I barely noticed the man and son, until everyone in ear shot noticed him as he began hollering and chasing the truck. The little boy had put the truck in gear, and it was rolling out of the gas station onto the highway into high-speed traffic. Many onlookers joined in the hot pursuit. One man, unable to stop the truck, ran to the road and started desperately flailing his arms to stop traffic. The entire scene was heart stopping. I recall the father's plea, "*God! Help me!*" When the truck finally stopped safely in the ravine on the other side of the highway, the man pulled his son from the truck and fell to his knees, embracing him and thanking everyone and Jesus for the help. His camo could not disguise his tears of mixed anguish, relief, and belief.

From without, he stood seconds away from horrific tragedy. We watched the trembling man buckle the boy into his car seat and make a beeline for the Dairy Queen. I can't know for sure, but experience (the subconscious of a seasoned mama) would bet he bought the boy a triple Texas-sized dipped cone and begged his son,

“*Please* don’t tell your mother about this.”

I don’t know this man; I saw him in his lack and panic. And he called upon his God. Perhaps this event taught his subconscious something about the name of God. Or maybe, if the story is ever relayed and he doesn’t take the tale with him to the grave, he will credit good citizens with saving his boy.

From without, we often beg God; from within, the conscious uses reason and concludes that was probably man’s effectiveness. And that is only fair; good people came to the desperate man’s aid. That makes sense to a traumatized man’s mind. But I propose it also further convinces the subconscious that we are provided for from outside of ourselves. If no one were there to help him and traffic parted like the Red Sea, the subconscious would have been left to believe that the God it could not see saved the boy.

In that instance, the subconscious, the heart—or deep beliefs—would have been given whole proof that the Lord provides. Who among us doesn’t crave this proof of the provision (Mark 9:24)? I believe if you have read this far, you want the mystery and romance of a God who always saves to be the restful, whole proof of a safe landing.

Still, we are asked to believe, have faith in the things hoped for, and if we ask, knowing in our heart (subconscious) we have received, the Lord does provide.

Maybe this was easier for Abraham, having been witness to the birth of a promised son by his elderly wife, Sarah. As the story goes, Abraham waited and hoped for a son long past the days of reasonable hope.

His belief counted him righteous, and the impossible was made real when, at the ripe old age of one hundred, his wife, Sarah, finally gave birth to a son, Isaac. Scripture tells us in Genesis 22 that later God said to him, "Hey! Abraham!"

"Here I am," Abraham replied. And God said, "Take your son, your only son, Isaac, *whom you love*, and go to the region of Moriah. Sacrifice him there as a burnt offering on one of the mountains I will tell you about."

Early the next morning, Abraham got up, saddled his donkey, took two of his servants, his son, Isaac, enough wood for the burnt offering, and set out for the place God had told him about.

The third day, Abraham looked up and saw the place in the distance. He said to his servants, "Stay here with the donkey while me and the boy go up there where we will worship." Abraham took the wood for the burnt offering and placed it on Isaac. As the two of them went off together, Isaac spoke up and said to his father, "Hey, Dad?"

"Yes, my son?"

"The fire and wood are here," Isaac said, "but where is the lamb for the burnt offering?"

Abraham answered, "God Himself will provide the lamb for the burnt offering, my son."

When they reached the place God had told him about, Abraham built an altar and arranged the wood on it. He bound his son and laid him on the altar on top of the wood. Then he reached out his hand and took the knife to slay his son. But the angel of the LORD called out to him from heaven, "Abraham! Abraham!"

And Abraham said, "Here I am."

"Do not lay a hand on the boy," the angel said. "Do not do anything to him! *I swear by myself,* declares the LORD, that because you have done this and have not withheld your son, your only son, I will surely bless you and make your descendants as numerous as the stars in the sky and as the sand on the seashore."

Abraham looked up, and there in a thicket, he saw a ram caught by its horns. He went over and took the ram and sacrificed it as a burnt offering instead of his son. So, Abraham called that place The LORD Will Provide. And to this day it is said, "On the mountain of the LORD it will be provided."

That is the short version with a little Jami-ness translation. In the long, exact version, I can't help but wonder, on the way back down the mountain, did Abraham also say, "Hey, son, if we could not tell your mother about this, I will buy you some ice cream."

Scripture doesn't tell us that Abraham grieved or toiled over the morbid task before him. It just shows us that Abraham was so fully convinced God always does what He says He will, that he decided to do whatever God asked with unshakable faith.

In this day and age, where proof of the world's power to save is a mere Google search away, it is easier to fall into the trap of crediting miracles to the world outside ourselves. From without, we are constantly in search of tangible solutions that we can make sense of. I am fully convinced, I feel it in my bones, we can change our minds about the power from within.

And I am not suggesting that you will ever be asked to

slaughter a child—sacrifice is not part of our faith walk. The only Sacrifice of value to God has been made. You may be asked to wait, or the answer may be different than what you expected, but there is an answer, and it is within you as you read.

From without, there will always be proof of lack. From within, there is greater proof when we continually remind the subconscious "Believe this, *feel* the thanksgiving, we can rest, the Lord has already provided." Like a soothing lullaby, my subconscious recites, "Not from without, from within," more and more often.

I said earlier that I have become more aware of the difference between the voice of my conscious mind and subconscious mind. I only recently noticed I was entertaining a weary thought, and it wasn't the familiar sounds of my subconscious. It was the smaller, less convincing part of my mind that was in doubt. I was overjoyed to realize that my subconscious was reciting, "Rest. It is not from without, it is from within."

This book is the most "teach-y" book I have written. I know the tone is a bit different than my others, and I have toiled with what readers will think. But this is a place of doubt that is created from without. Without knowing what to expect from the world, I project my worst-case, past experience, positive or negative reviews, or numbers that don't jive onto readers who have not read it yet, and I am left in unrest. From within, I know, these words were inspired. They were written with love, and everything that comes up after this is placed in the hands of readers is already provided for from within.

Projection is a stumbling block in our deep beliefs. It reasons and creates from without in the hopes of preserving the sanity within. However, throwing all the outside junk to the curb and rehearsing the words "Not from without, but from within," I need not wait on the world's answers. The Lord has already provided a way.

Projecting onto others is an entirely different kind of mess. You have just read hundreds of words that divulge my thoughts, but you cannot wholly count on knowing every single thing about me, even if we spent ten years in each other's company. Not even my parents or Justin can decipher everything that I am on the basis of our human relationship, without projecting some of who they are onto me. We are unique in our creation. And we are wholly known by our Creator.

To fully know Him in return, our subconscious must be convinced of His presence and power from within. And it will listen to you. It works with you in tandem to stay alive and be at rest when the internal no longer battles itself from without and rests fully in the power of Truth from within.

Furthermore, the space where we recall that this God who dwells within died "for that too" ceases to project brokenness on others. It decides and wrestles judgment out of our minds and morphs it into love. We become who He asked us to be without conflict. We no longer must struggle with what someone may or may not think. When we are deciding with God from within, love is the correct answer. Others may argue, but we are at rest.

As I close, I am taken aback by my feelings. I am not

weeping or afraid. I remember quite vividly what it was like to finish my first book—the imagined terrors of the publishing world clawing for acclaim. My second book about my journey as a mom was soggy from the tears of the past and wild future yet to be reined in by my feeble work. My third, a journey to freedom from a life of self-loathing, left me crumpled on the bathroom floor, anguished relief escaping from me in hysterical sobs. And here, in this space, as the words *The End* begged to be typed, I am overcome with joy and rest.

Will it read well? I hope so. Will you laugh? Cry? Curse? Spit? Fall to your knees and rest? Of course, I cannot know. I have hopes, dreams, and goals. I still run out of eggs and milk. In the course of my studies, I read a quote in one of Luke's hippie books: "Before enlightenment, chop wood, carry water. After enlightenment, chop wood, carry water."[12] At the time, I ignored it. But from this place of rest, I now know it is of relevance.

John 16:33 says it in words I can better digest. Jesus said, "I have told you these things, so that in me you may have peace. In this world you will have trouble. But take heart! I have overcome the world."

Now, all that is left is rest not from without. . .but from within.

Go in peace and rest, believing it is finished.

Jesus be all over you.

Love, Jami

12 Patrick Allan, "Four 'Confusing' Zen Quotes and What You Can Learn from Them," Lifehacker, December 30, 2014, https://lifehacker.com/four-confusing-zen-quotes-and-what-you-can-learn-from-1676177538

Afterword

Having finished a little ahead of schedule, I decided to surprise Justin and the boys and come home one day early. I placed my suitcase on the luggage cart and felt the pangs of frustration.

My suitcase is only about a year old. It is beautiful. It is a shiny hard-shell, charcoal gray, with huge red tea roses, purple jasmine blooms, and olive-green vines. It has a retractable pull that telescopes to different comfortable heights and crafty swivel wheels. I can buzz through airports in record time.

People stop me to ask about my beautiful suitcase. I love that suitcase. . .*but. . .*

It has no handles. It has the telescoping pull and no handles, not on top, not on the side. I would rather have Sophie's burnt-orange suitcase than my beautiful floral one. So, while I can put tons of things in it, the hard shell protects my belongings from damage, and it is easy to push or pull, I can't lift it.

Well, I can, but it is a heavy task. Imagine picking up a forty-gallon barrel of water in bear-hug fashion, and you can picture me trying to maneuver this suitcase in and out of my vehicle or on and off a luggage carousel. It is nearly impossible and always awkward. The beauty of the suitcase is lost on the heavy burden of no handles.

Had it not been such a backbreaking task, I would have unloaded everything, checked back into the hotel, and taken a nap. By the time I wrestled the handleless beast into my car, I was out of breath, bruised, and exhausted.

If I lacked an ounce of confidence in Jesus, here is where He showed up again.

The fancy-looking luggage reminded me that our faith is complete. It is not just shiny and pretty to look at with no tangible value. It has all the bells and whistles, all the love and rest, all the loveliness, and all the function. We can drag it behind us, adjusting it to make it easier to maneuver, and some might stop to inquire about it.

However, if we do not embrace or understand all the parts, it is simply the shell that looks nice. It is just a big bag of unrest. We carry the burden of have-tos, can'ts, and wants, wishing for more. If the suitcase had handles, why would I pick it up like I am moving a barrel of hayseed?

My dad is a geologist. As a girl, I took fossils and fancy rocks from his collection to show and tell. Once a little girl raised her hand and said, "I don't believe in that stuff. I believe in Jesus." I was standing there holding a trilobite fossil. I could have thrown it and hit her with it. The fossil was as real as she was. To not believe in what you can get pummeled with in the name of faith confuses the mind. Just like we can experience rest in grief, we can live the entirety of our faith and still understand dinosaurs roamed the earth.

All the advances in science, mind research, and the God who designed them, the stars, and gravity are yours. It is not a religion or denomination. It is not meant to weigh you down or break your back. It is not just a show or the nearest convenience, a quick ticket to heaven.

It is all that He promised, no buts.

He doesn't lack a thing. And neither do you.

Rest, Girl. . .it is well.

About the Author

Jami Amerine is an author, speaker, artist, wife, and mom. She and her husband, Justin, live in Houston, Texas, and have six children. She holds a master's of education in Counseling & Human Development. Jami and Justin are advocates for foster care and adoption. Jami blogs at sacredgroundstickyfloors.com

Acknowledgments

Thank You, Jesus. Thank You for loving perfectly, loving wholly, and rising that I might live in rest.

To Justin, keeper of my heart, bringer of my coffee. You don't complete me, but you sure make my life a heck of a great love story.

To Maggie, Christian, John, Anne, Luke, Sophie, Sam, and Charlie, I love you and I like you. You have taught me many truths about true love and provided me some great content.

To John and Bosco. . .what if?

To my mom and dad, you are both my beloved parents and dear friends.

To Stacey, Dean, Michael, Kelly, the vandals and the pixies, I love you each.

To Katie M. Reid, having arrived with you in this space of rest is one of the greatest pleasures I can recall. Thank you so much for your wisdom, insight, love, compassion, and genius. You are my favorite Martha and cherished friend.

To Adam Reid, thank you for sharing Katie and

encouraging, discerning, and teaching with such passion, compassion, and wisdom.

To Carey Scott, I like you. Thank you for being my friend through thick and thin, together and alone.

To Blakely Berring, there are no coincidences; you are proof of God in everything and everywhere and in everyone, just in time.

To Lorraine Reep, with every trial, you speak truth and radiate grace. I am eternally grateful for our friendship and all that you and Mike are and do in the name of love.

To Jeane Burgess, love turns work into rest. . .and many times, love turns work into one of the best friends a girl can have.

And to the many friends who have continued to walk with me, encourage, and love me—Kim Phelan, Marcy Toppert, Susannah B. Lewis, Emily Potter, Shelby Spear, Christine Carter, Michelle Hedrick, Tracy Steel, Alexa Carlton, Sarah Bennet, and Kandy Chimento, I love you girls.

To my literary agent, Dave Schroeder, thank you for partnering in my often-exhausting ideas with wisdom and vision.

And to Barbour Publishing, Annie, Kelly, Shalyn, and all the gang. You are a delight to create with. Jesus be all over you.

ALSO FROM JAMI AMERINE. . .

Well, Girl

If you're skinny, fat, short, tall, or somewhere in between. . .
If you've ever thought that losing weight
would lead to happiness. . .
If you've ever avoided a mirror because
you didn't want to see your reflection. . .
If you've found Jesus or you're still searching. . .
Well, Girl, you've come to the right place.

You'll find a sassy, funny, authentic, and encouraging friend in master word-weaver Jami Amerine, as she comes alongside you to share God's overwhelming grace and patience in an inside-out journey to wellness. She'll introduce you to a heavenly Father who adores you, right where you are. And she'll let you have a peek into the insane ride of her life that led her to complete freedom after years of hating herself—while she was completely and utterly adored by Jesus.

This transformational read will set you free. Hilarious, raw, and poetic, *Well, Girl* offers scriptural truths, honest and thought-provoking ideas about wellness, and an in-depth look at a life free from culture's lies—with increased self-worth, better overall health, and more confidence in your physical appearance.

Paperback / 978-1-64352-558-7 / $14.99